PLUNDER & PILLAGE

ATLANTIC CANADA'S BRUTAL & BLOODTHIRSTY PIRATES & PRIVATEERS

HAROLD HORWOOD

FORMAC PUBLISHING COMPANY LIMITED
HALIFAX

Formac Publishing Company Limited recognizes the support of the Province of Nova Scotia through the Department of Tourism, Culture and Heritage. We acknowledge the financial support of the Government of Canada through the Canada Book Fund for our publishing activities. We acknowledge the support of the Canada Council for the Arts, which last year invested $20.1 million in writing and publishing throughout Canada.

Cover image: iStockphoto

Library and Archives Canada Cataloguing in Publication

Horwood, Harold, 1923-2006
        Plunder and pillage : Atlantic Canada's brutal and bloodthirsty pirates and privateers / Harold Horwood.

Includes bibliographical references and index.
Issued also in an electronic format.
ISBN 978-0-88780-949-1

        1. Pirates — Atlantic Coast (Canada) — History.
2. Privateering — Atlantic Coast (Canada) — History.
I. Title.

FC2019.P57H67 2011   909'.096344   C2010-907935-3

Formac Publishing Company Limited
5502 Atlantic Street
Halifax, Nova Scotia, Canada B3H 1G4
www.formac.ca

Printed and bound in Canada.

Distributed in the United States by:
Casemate Publishers and Book
Distributors, L.L.C.
908 Darby Road
Havertown, PA
19083

Distributed in the United Kingdom by:
Casemate UK
17 Cheap Street
Newbury, Berkshire
RG14 5OD

CONTENTS

ACKNOWLEDGEMENTS

THE AUTHOR WOULD like to thank the following institutions: the Public Archives of Newfoundland, Nova Scotia, Prince Edward Island, the Public Archives of Massachusetts; the Public Archives and National Library of Canada; the British Public Records Office; the Gosling Memorial Library, St. John's; the Conception Bay Museum, Harbour Grace; the Maritime Museum, Boston; the New Brunswick Museum; the Newfoundland Historical Society; Department of the Navy, Naval Historical Centre, Washington D.C.; Library of Congress, Washington D.C. A special note of thanks to Mr. Dwight Girty.

INTRODUCTION

PIRACY IS OLDER THAN HISTORY. The ships of Ancient Egypt had to defend themselves against sea rovers; pirates seized the young Julius Caesar and held him for ransom. They played a major role — perhaps the decisive one — in bringing to an end the great Norse venture to Greenland and America in the five centuries before Columbus. The Greenland colonies, founded so long before by Eric the Red, were repeatedly sacked early in the fifteenth century by English and Scottish pirates who carried off Greenlanders to be sold as slaves in the Muslim lands of North Africa.

The great age of piracy in the Atlantic coincided with the colonizing of the New World by Europeans. The Spanish colonies, in particular, were little more than centres for the gathering of loot from older and richer civilizations such as those of the Incas and the Aztecs. Since this loot had to be convoyed across the Atlantic to Spain, and since the English, French, and Dutch had by that time learned to build ships that were faster, nimbler, and better armed than anything owned by the Spaniards, the Spanish treasure ships offered a tempting and easy target for pirates and privateers from northwestern Europe.

The distinction between a pirate and a privateer was simply that the privateer sailed with the blessing of his government to capture enemy ships, either in wartime or in a part of the world that his government regarded as no-man's land, while the pirate sailed under no greater authority than that of his own guns. The privateer carried letters of marque authorizing him to prey on the ships of certain nations. England, in the sixteenth and seventeenth centuries, made the curious distinction that even when she was at peace with Spain she might still be at war with the Spanish colonies in the New World. After all, the Spaniards were in the Caribbean by authority of the Pope, and the Pope, in newly Protestant England, had no authority. So the reasoning went — an excuse for allowing Drake, Hawkins, and their successors to prey on Spanish ships and Spanish colonies even when Spain and England were not at war.

It is interesting to question just who should and who should not be classified as a pirate. Francis Drake, the arch-pirate El Draco of Spanish history, plundered the Spanish colonies of the New World with a privateering commission issued by the great Queen Elizabeth of England and was rewarded with a knighthood. In Spain, El

Draco is remembered as the most vicious pirate in history — the Ghengis Khan of the freebooters; in England he is remembered as Sir Francis Drake, the greatest hero of the Elizabethan Age. Sometimes the distinction was so fine that a privateer might stray into piracy almost by accident. This seems to be what happened to Captain William Kidd, who began life as a respectable naval officer, commanded the most splendid privateer of his time with a commission from Great Britain to police the Indian Ocean, but ended his life on the gallows as a pirate in 1701. There is still a lively debate among historians as to whether Captain Kidd was ever guilty of piracy at all. Though the distinction should have been simple, it wasn't always so, and it was sometimes a question of what you could get away with. If you succeeded, all might be forgiven. If you failed, you might be hanged, drawn and quartered, or broken on the wheel.

This book follows the fortunes of several such characters who preyed upon the shipping and coast of Atlantic Canada from the seventeenth to the nineteenth century. The story starts in 1611 with the arch-pirate Peter Easton, a folk hero in Newfoundland, and ends in 1865 with Mogul Mackenzie, a privateer who seems to have turned to piracy, and who disappeared without a trace in the Bay of Fundy. In between are the stories of an assortment of pirates and privateers, some of whom fall into both camps.

Hard on the heels of the Spanish thrust into Central America came the English, French, and Portuguese fisheries in Newfoundland and Nova Scotia. The fisheries quickly mushroomed into an immense industry, employing hundreds of ships and tens of thousands of men and women in a land with no government closer than Europe and no

authority higher than that of the "fishing admirals" — the
first captain to arrive at a port in the spring became "admiral" of that port for the year. So Newfoundland became
the very nest from which pirates were hatched. The pirate
captains set up forts, careenages, and docks; they recruited
shipwrights, sailmakers, iron-workers, and deckhands by
the thousands; then they sailed south, well equipped to deal
with the merchant ships of all nations, including their own.

Although the taking of the Spanish treasure ship was the
grand slam of piracy, other smaller victories were welcomed
— French cargoes of wine, English cargoes of shore-cured
fish, and, a little later, cargoes of furs from Hudson Bay and
the St. Lawrence River. The dukedoms of southern France
ran a massive black market. One could sell anything, including captured ships, in the French "free ports." One could do
almost as well, with no greater risk, in Ireland and western
England, where robber barons commanded armed castles
only loosely attached to the English Crown. These barons
became the great outfitters and protectors of the English
pirates, investing in pirate voyages without risk to themselves and having the means to dispose of whatever cargoes
the pirates brought home.

The glittering reward, the great hope that lured men
into piracy, was wealth, with its attendant power and ease.
In the seventeenth century, when the story of piracy in
Canada begins, the annual wage for a working man ranged
from five to ten pounds sterling. But the payoff at the end
of a pirate voyage was often a thousand pounds or more —
enough to buy an estate or, prudently invested, to support
one's family in comfort for life. A common pirate might
rise from deckhand ("scum," as their officers called them)

to country squire. A pirate captain might rise much higher. Three of the Newfoundland pirates bought their way into the European nobility.

Piracy was a much more complex trade than mere brigandage. To practise it successfully one needed a ship, preferably well armed, a navigator, and a large crew. Pirates captured their prizes, as a rule, by sheer weight of numbers. A merchant crew facing a boarding party that might outnumber them ten to one had little choice but to surrender. If they surrendered without a fight, their lives would usually be spared. Often they would have the choice of joining the pirates or sailing away naked in an empty ship.

The pirates depended upon constant recruitment, often at sea. Bristol, in the seventeenth and eighteenth centuries, was the world capital of both piracy and the slave trade, a port that eclipsed even London in the volume of its commerce. But even there a pirate captain could not boldly recruit a crew of a hundred fighting men and clear "for the high seas." Rather, he left on a peaceful trading or fishing voyage and then "went on the account." This phrase, meaning "turned pirate," was derived from "going off on your own account," in other words, working for yourself instead of for a shipowner.

Merchant ships carried only a handful of men and boys — ten to twenty — depending on the size of the ship. Fishing ships might carry twice that number, including two or three women and several "Irish youngsters" shipping out as servants in the fishery. So, when a captain and crew went on the account, the first thing they needed was more men — hence the everlasting recruitment of fishing crews and the astonishing numbers of Newfoundland fishermen reported to have sailed away as pirates.

There was always the risk of being caught and hanged — pirates were still sometimes hanged in the seventeenth century — but the risk was no longer a very grave one. Governments, especially of Great Britain, often issued general pardons to allow wayward seamen to come home and man the fleets once more. If war broke out, as it frequently did, whole flotillas of pirates would volunteer as privateers, with all past sins forgiven. Anyone rich enough could almost always buy immunity from the tolerant kings of England or France or even Spain — the Spaniards were not above hiring foreign pirates to help them compete in their losing struggle for maritime supremacy with their northern rivals. But the one thing a common jack pirate with no saleable skills needed to avoid was falling into the hands of the Spaniards, who had a nasty habit of burning pirates alive as heretics or working them to death as plantation or galley slaves.

It was a young man's game. Most pirates ranged between the ages of eighteen and thirty. A few older men went on the account, but most either died or retired before middle age. Boys as young as ten were repeatedly listed as members of pirate crews and sometimes escaped hanging because of their youth (only to be sent to the plantations as indentured labour or, in one case, to be reprieved from hanging and imprisoned for ten years). The pirates, too, seem to have pitied these waifs of the high seas. In one shareout of pirate plunder, all boys under the age of sixteen were allotted one hundred pounds each "to enable them to apprentice themselves to an honest trade ashore."

By the late seventeenth century the major pirate black markets had shifted from the old world to the new. Ireland, Cornwall, and the Riviera now gave place to the capitals of the English overseas colonies. Sir David Kirke, who captured Quebec from Champlain and was awarded the governorship of Newfoundland, made his capital, Ferryland, into a free port for the sale of pirate loot and a major centre in the rum trade.

The Navigation Acts that, in effect, tried to force the British colonies to trade with Britain alone encouraged smuggling and piracy. By the 1670s, colonial governors from New England to the Carolinas were outfitting pirates and openly entertaining them in their mansions and, at times, even issuing letters of marque (for which they had no authority) to protect the pirates from any king's ship they might chance to meet. Such governors were often recalled by outraged British officials, but just as often were replaced by men equally corruptible — the pirates found that almost every governor had his price.

Piracy was a grave problem to the colonies that eventually became Canada, and issuing letters of marque and reprisal was one way to deal with it. Privateering against pirates was an ancient institution, even then. The first Vice-Admiralty Court outside the realm of England was set up at Trinity in Newfoundland in 1615, to deal with piracy in the New World. In 1620, the Duke of Buckingham, Lord Admiral of England, issued a commission to John Mason, governor of the Cupids colony in Newfoundland, and to Captain William Bushell, to "take up and press such ships with mariners, soldiers, gunners, munitions of war, stores, etc. as may be necessary for the purpose of suppressing pirates and Sea Rovers." They were commissioned specifically to set forth in "the good ship *Peter and Andrew* of London of 320 tons burthen" for Newfoundland with such men and ordnance as they needed for the purpose of taking pirates and their ships. Their pay was to be possession of one half the value of the pirate ships they captured.

From this commission it is obvious that privateering companies were authorized to use press gangs to recruit their crews. But such highhandedness was never popular in the colonies, and by the late years of the eighteenth century privateering captains, or other agents of companies in the business, were relying exclusively on volunteers. These men signed contracts of service, guaranteeing each one a share of the loot. Under the terms of one such contract a cabin boy walked off with an incredible fortune of more than £1,000, a sum that he would have been lucky to earn after fifty years of honest toil.

Despite such commissions for the suppression of piracy, no really effective remedy was found until the Royal Navy began patrolling the high seas with fast sloops-of-war especially fitted out for capturing pirates. This action, carried out in the latter part of the eighteenth century, was effective for a while, until the American War of Independence, the Wars of Napoleon, and the War of 1812 set off privateering on a massive scale, with many of the privateers slipping into piracy when their letters of marque expired. Piracy in the Atlantic was not finally suppressed until well into the second half of the nineteenth century. In Canada the last hanging for piracy was in Halifax in 1809, but other Canadian pirates were hanged for murder or retired. One didn't die until 1870, long after piracy had disappeared from Canadian seas.

Privateers were a major force in early Canada. Even before the Cartier voyages, when the records are scanty indeed, there is enough to show that privateers helped to determine which nations should benefit from the all-important New World fisheries and the less important, but growing, trade in furs. Jacques Cartier himself, who explored the Gulf of St. Lawrence in 1534 with a commission from the King of France, is believed by historians to have been a privateer — perhaps even a pirate — before becoming a respectable explorer. Privateering was also vital in Britain's wars against New France. It prevented the infant United States from being crushed by British regulars and enriched the maritime colonies in the Napoleonic Wars. Finally, it saved Canada from conquest in the War of 1812.

The first great privateering voyage to what is now Canada was fitted out by Jean Ango of Havre de Grace, the most powerful sea lord of his time, sailing under letters of marque from the King of France. In 1520, a mere twenty-three years after the first Cabot voyage, Ango sent a squadron to Newfoundland commanded by two brothers named Parmentier. Already there was a thriving Newfoundland fishery with Spanish, Portuguese, Basque, French, and English ships making annual voyages. The Parmentier brothers captured and looted the ships of all nations except the French. They also sacked and burned whatever fishing premises they could find ashore. They named the port of Havre de Grace in Conception Bay after the port their patron had founded in France. Anglicized, later, to Harbour Grace, it became a pirate stronghold in the seventeenth century and a great fishing and trading centre in the nineteenth. Eventually it was the second-largest centre of population, after St. John's. Ango continued to send armed ships to the Newfoundland fishery for some twenty years, acting as escorts for French fishing ships and with a licence to plunder the ships of other nations. His privateering expeditions had the effect of making France the ascendant power in the New World fisheries for almost half a century, until the English began to take control in the 1570s.

Privateers were commissioned to capture enemy property and interfere with enemy commerce, not to destroy human life. Their aim was to capture ships with as little damage as possible, for the sale of such ships, with their cargoes, was the privateersman's sole hope of reward. They preferred to attack unarmed or lightly armed merchantmen, presenting them, when possible, with overwhelming odds, if not in guns, then at least in manpower. In this way they could usually secure a surrender without bloodshed.

Privateering was, therefore, a far less dangerous trade than service in the navy, and was a favourite refuge from naval conscription: by enlisting on a privateer you might hope to escape the navy with its hardships, harsh discipline, and high risk. Though the privateers were just as overcrowded as any man-of-war, there was little danger of being hanged or flogged to death and only slight danger of being killed in action. Even the famous slugging matches, when broadsides were exchanged almost rail-to-rail and masts went crashing over the side, often resulted in few casualties: a man or two killed, one or two wounded was typical. Casualties in these battles generally depended on how the ships fired their guns. Raking decks with grapeshot, designed to kill the crew, was not a favoured tactic; between honourable opponents it was a contemptible way to fight. You didn't aim at the waterline, trying to sink your enemy either. You aimed at the rigging, hoping to disable the ship and force her to surrender in a condition fit for repair — and eventual resale.

We have to thank the science of marine archaeology for our knowledge of what the raiders of the early sixteenth century were like. Wrecks of some of the ships that sailed as pirates and privateers in the earliest days of New World settlement have been recovered, and it is obvious that even in those days ships were being built specifically for the job of privateering. Looking more like the Viking ships of earlier centuries, they bore little resemblance to either the merchant ships or the warships of their time. In the sixteenth century the warship was a real monster, beautifully portrayed in detailed paintings of the time, with as many as seven decks piled one above another, projecting far over bow and stern and appropriately called "castles." They were floating forts, and they were almost as top-heavy as they looked. They rarely ventured far from land and would certainly not have attempted a transatlantic voyage. Merchant ships were built like barges, with round bows and round sterns, as much beam as possible, and could travel at a speed, with a good following wind, of perhaps five or six knots.

The privateer was something quite different from either of these. Though she might run between one hundred and two hundred tons, she had a narrow racing hull and pointed bow and stern, with light timbering. She was rigged with lateen sails that could be spread wing-and-wing in a following wind or close-hauled for sailing much closer to a head wind than any merchant ship or warship. She was armed with a couple of long bow-chasers to make her effective at a distance and with rows of swivel guns along each side for close-in fighting. She was built for action, an ideal ship for piracy as well as the somewhat more reputable profession of privateering.

The privateer was often a rich merchant and, at least in later times, was supposed to respect international rules of warfare. But to the privateer's victim he was often a pirate and sometimes a criminal just as vicious as Blackbeard or any other freebooter of the Spanish Main. Some of the privateers encountered in this book played by the rules. Others raped women, looted private homes, murdered defenceless farmers, and took the scalps of aboriginal children.

Such men, sometimes heroic, sometimes pitiable, sometimes unrelievedly vicious, are the substance of this book, their lives wrapped up in the blood, the violence, and the terror that have been edited out of Canada's past. The Canadian establishment has rarely admitted that Canada has a violent history. They have created the myth of the "rule of law" right from the day General Wolfe "planted firm Britannia's flag on Canada's fair domain," allowing them to look down their long blue noses at the barbaric Americans. We tend to romanticize and civilize our past. In fact, the age of gunpowder was not a comfortable age in which to live in coastal Nova Scotia, New Brunswick, Prince Edward Island, Quebec, or Newfoundland, with shiploads of drunken thugs out to rob you and burn your house, or if you were an aboriginal, ship you off as a slave to the West Indian sugar plantations.

Here, then, are the stories of some of the men who, during the past four centuries, plundered and pillaged the shipping and coastal settlements of Atlantic Canada.

CHAPTER 1
THE GREAT EASTON

I N THE YEAR 1611 Samuel Champlain was struggling
to found his tiny colony at Quebec, Henry Hudson was
adrift in a boat, cast away by his mutinous crew in the
great bay that would later bear his name, and Port Royal, in
southern Nova Scotia, was languishing, virtually abandoned,
because the colony was bankrupt.

But in the land that would later become Canada, trade
and commerce were booming in at least one place. In
Newfoundland some ten thousand men (and a few women)
with three hundred and fifty to four hundred ships carried
on the greatest fishing enterprise the world had ever seen.

The New Founde Land (which then included Labrador, the
Gulf of St. Lawrence, and most of Nova Scotia) was claimed

by England but was host to the ships of several nations. St. John's, its principal harbour and centre of commerce, was a free port where Basques, Portuguese, French, and English traded their goods and refitted their ships.

In those days even the humblest fishing ship went armed with at least a few cannons or swivel guns, since dried and salted fish was an immensely valuable cargo. A shipload might sell for a thousand pounds sterling at a time when one pound was a generous month's wages for a tradesman. So there was constant danger that both ship and cargo would be hijacked and sold in the French free ports, the independent dukedoms of the Riviera that at that time ran the world's largest black market and carried on a lively trade with the Muslim kingdoms across the Mediterranean in North Africa.

Into the anarchy of the Newfoundland fishery there descended, in the summer of 1611, an agent of law and order who recognized no authority higher than his own but had both the force and the will to impose a kind of government. This was Captain Peter Easton, the pirate admiral in command of ten strong ships of war, who flew from the masthead of his flagship, the *Happy Adventure*, not some fanciful rag of a skull and crossbones later flown by minor cutthroats like Blackbeard, but the red-and-white cross of St. George, the flag that Drake and Raleigh and Gilbert had carried across the oceans a few years before.

Easton was an English gentleman and from an old family that had produced a bishop in the twelfth century. The Eastons had fought in the Crusades and, much later, against the Spanish Armada. In the great days of Queen Elizabeth I they had taken to seafaring, like so many other prominent families, and one of them had been master of the *Sunshine*, flagship of the Davis expedition that sailed in search of the Northwest Passage in 1585.

Peter Easton had visited Newfoundland as early as 1602, when Elizabeth was still on the throne of England and was still engaged in hit-and-run warfare at sea with the King of Spain. Much of this warfare and some of the convoy duty for England's commercial fleets were carried on by privateers, ships owned and fitted out by private citizens, most of them wealthy aristocrats, and carrying the Queen's commission to prey on the shipping of her enemies.

On that occasion Easton sailed as convoy for the Newfoundland fishing fleet, and on the outward voyage he liberated from a Dutch privateer an Irish girl named Sheila O'Connor, known in Newfoundland ever since as "the Irish Princess" or "Sheila Nagira." ("Nagira" is not a surname, but a corruption of an old Gaelic word meaning "The Beautiful.") Sheila had married one of Easton's lieutenants, a young man named Gilbert Pike. They became planters at the settlement of Mosquito, now called Bristol's Hope, and founded the very large family of Newfoundland Pikes.

A planter was not someone who planted crops but someone who planted a business enterprise of some kind in a colony — in the case of Newfoundland, planters owned fishing premises and boats and employed either servants or sharemen in the shore fishery.

On that first visit to Newfoundland Peter Easton had the legal right to requisition stores, munitions, even seamen if he needed them, from the fishing fleets. On his second visit he behaved in the same way with not a shred of legal authority. The privateer had become the world's most powerful pirate.

There had been a massive transition from privateering

to piracy in 1603 when Elizabeth died and was succeeded by King James I. He promptly made peace with Spain, cancelled all letters of marque carried by privateers, and laid up the vessels of his own fleet. Men who had served in the navy kept their rank but ceased to draw pay from the royal exchequer. Men who had served as privateers and had lived by legal plunder now found themselves unemployed and wholly unfitted for a life of honest toil. Many of them turned to piracy. This happened, for example, with the captains who had sailed in the fleets of Elizabeth's favourite, Sir Walter Raleigh. They are euphemistically described as "erring captains" by the chroniclers of James's reign.

There were three classes of such pirates — those who attacked only the ships of their former enemies, the Spanish (and perhaps the Dutch, who were Spanish vassals), those who attacked ships of any foreign power, and those who attacked anything, including the ships of England.

Easton seems to have belonged to the third class. He wielded such power that he rarely had to shoot it out with anybody, but he certainly took supplies and seamen, if not cargoes, from English shipping and seems to have levied fees for free passage through the English Channel — at least, that seems to have been the complaint of the West Country merchants in a petition to the Lord Admiral explaining that they were forced to pay "protection" money, a kind of toll, to ensure safe passage in and out of such ports as Poole and Bristol.

By 1610 Easton commanded a fleet of forty ships that controlled all traffic through the English Channel. Just how firm a control he exercised over this fleet is open to question. Most of the pirate captains must have been fairly independent, but they were beholden to aristocratic patrons ashore, especially to the Killigrews, the "Robber Barons of Land's End," who were financiers and brokers for the pirates and gave them safe haven in the fourteen miles of navigable water that lay inland from their great fortress, Pendennis Castle, in Cornwall. The Killigrews, in turn, regarded Easton as their principal agent at sea, and he was, if not exactly a pirate admiral, at least the recognized leader of a loose federation of pirates.

The Killigrews were always well connected at Court. One of them had been Elizabeth's Foreign Minister. Another was Groom of Her Bedchamber. A third was Master of the Revels (to James), and a fourth became a desk admiral. But their loyalty to the Crown was loose and self-serving. One of the Killigrews even tried to sell England to the Spanish invaders for ten thousand gold crowns and was tried for treason but was eventually acquitted and restored to favour.

In 1610 the Bristol merchants presented a petition to Lord Nottingham, head of King James's paper navy, begging for relief from Easton's depredations. Nottingham replied by commissioning a daring young man named Henry Mainwaring (pronounced "Mannering") to go in pursuit of Easton and bring him to London.

Mainwaring, aged twenty-three, was a scholar, soldier, sailor, lawyer, and politician, an aristocrat a step higher on the social scale than Easton — a typical Elizabethan born a generation too late. When he discovered that the ships offered to him by Nottingham were worm-eaten and unsea-worthy from seven years of disuse, he fitted out his own squadron, headed by his own ship, the *Princess*, presumably at his own expense and at the expense of his friends.

This gave Easton plenty of time to decide what to do. He had news, through the Killigrews, of everything that went on in government, and they doubtless advised him to make a foreign voyage. Giving battle to Mainwaring within the "Narrow Seas" might be interpreted as making war on the King, treason within the realm, as it was called. So he sailed for the Coast of Guinea — the long bight of Africa that was the source of ivory, gold, and slaves — and thence to Newfoundland, where he arrived in 1611 with ten ships of war "well furnished and very rich," as Sir Richard Whitbourne described them in his *Discourse and Discovery of the New-Found-Land*.

Whitbourne, who spent his working life in Newfoundland from 1579 to 1619, rising from a ship's mate to a vice-admiralty court judge and finally to a knighthood, was fishing admiral of the port of St. John's when Easton arrived and the closest thing Newfoundland had to a colonial governor. The pirate invited Whitbourne to visit him, and: "I was kept eleven weeks under his command, and had from him many golden promises, and much wealth offered to be put into my hands as is well known."

Whitbourne was entertained lavishly on Easton's flagship. They ate and drank in the comfort of the "great cabin" built at the stern between the main deck and the quarterdeck. It was the only decent living quarters anywhere on the ship, furnished with rugs, chairs, tables, cabinets, great lamps hung in gimbals, and instruments of navigation. There may also have been a glass-fronted case with books and a Bible. We do not know whether Easton carried a library in his ship, but other gentlemen-navigators of the time did and liked to sit on the quarterdeck in fair weather with a book of poetry in hand.

He is described as a dark man of athletic build and medium stature, but no portrait of him survives. He dressed like all gentlemen of his period, in doublet and hose, silver-buckled shoes, with fashionable cloak, sword, lace cuffs, and, more than likely, a feather in his hat.

The men who worked his ships loved and admired him — he was regarded as a great and generous leader. But between him and them there was a vast gap in status, appearance, and lifestyle. The seamen had no living quarters. They slept between decks among the guns, in a space where you couldn't stand straight because of lack of headroom. If they had hammocks, they slung them wherever they could. Otherwise, they slept on the deck boards.

They were universally barefooted and ill-clothed. Unlike gentlemen, who affected knee-breeches and silk stockings, the sailors wore trousers and little else. The trousers and a coarse shirt or jerkin were often made of sail canvas and were sometimes tarred to make them weatherproof. Pirates of a later day dressed in the captured clothing of their victims, but it seems unlikely that the tightly disciplined sailors who served under the aristocratic pirates of Easton's time did so.

The *Happy Adventure* was a ship of about 350 tons, double-decked and three-masted. In naval terms she might have been called a frigate, meaning something lighter than a full war galleon, with a rig similar, but not identical, to that of a merchant ship. She probably mounted thirty to forty full-sized cannons and any number of smaller swivel guns designed not for wrecking ships but for killing or maiming their crews when armed with canister and grapeshot and other such devilish devices. She would need about 150 men to work her properly in battle.

She was rigged with square sails, except for a large fore-and-aft or lateen sail at the stern. The advantage of the large fore-and-aft sail was that it made the ship more manoeuvrable than a full square-rigger and better able to sail close-hauled against the wind. In an age when fore-and-aft sails were still uncommon except on single-masted ships, the pirates had discovered and adopted this mixed rig, later to become standard on all the seven seas.

We might wonder why Captain Whitbourne, holding a vice-admiralty commission for the suppression of piracy (the first ever issued outside the realm of England), would allow himself to be "kept under the command" of a man like Easton. The answer lies in the bred-in-the-bone attitudes of the seventeenth century. Whitbourne, for all his authority among the fishing fleets, was a mere merchant who had risen from the working class, while Easton was an aristocrat, born to rule. Commoners crossed such men at their peril. They might be out of favour with the King this year, but one of his trusted councillors the next.

Easton's main purpose in Newfoundland was to recruit men, repair and reprovision his ships, and capture arms and ammunition, especially from French and Basque fishing ships, most of which would carry a few guns but not nearly enough to put up a fight against Easton's squadron. But while he was about this more serious business, he also took cargoes of salt fish from French and Portuguese ships and at least one cargo of French wine. Sir William Vaughan, who tried to found a colony near Cape Race, estimated that Easton's ships took out of Newfoundland 100 pieces of ordnance and 1500 mariners or fishermen, "to the great hurt of the Newfoundland plantations."

One of the letters from John Guy's colony at Cupids, dated 1612, reports Easton at Harbour Grace "trimming and repairing his shipping, and [hath] taken munitions, etc. together with about 100 men out of the bay, he purposeth to have 500 out of the land before he goeth."

The numbers recruited for pirate crews may seem exaggerated until we remember that Easton manned his ships with 180 men each (as reported by Guy) compared with the crew of 28 employed by Whitbourne at fishing.

But the London and Bristol Company that had founded the colony at Cupids was glad enough to accept the pirates' protection when it came to their stores. Fishery salt was always in short supply because the English had to get it in trade from France or Portugal, and in winter or early spring, when the colony was undermanned, their supplies would be vulnerable to thieves or raiders. So on October 12, 1612, John Guy's colonists landed at the pirates' fort in Harbour Grace and gave their fishing supplies, including fifteen tons of salt, into Easton's keeping for protection until the following spring.

Although Newfoundland was his home base from 1611 to 1614, Peter Easton's main interests lay far to the south where he could prey on Spanish shipping and even on English ships that he caught trading with the Spaniards. One such ship belonged to Captain Rashley of Foy in Cornwall. Easton captured it "upon the coast of Guinnie" where it was loading slaves for the Spanish colonies and took it to Newfoundland as a prize. But Whitbourne persuaded him to restore it to its owner, secured a freight for the vessel, and sent it home, "never having so much as thanks for my pains."

Easton's greatest coup during this period was a successful

raid on the Spanish colony at Puerto Rico, with its supposedly impregnable fort, Moro Castle, that had withstood an
attack by Sir Francis Drake. Easton apparently took the
colony by surprise and decamped with whatever stockpiles
of gold had been smelted from its famous mines. He also
brought home to Harbour Grace a Spanish ship, the *San
Sebastian*, reportedly stocked with treasure. This daring
raid gave him a reputation for invincibility that he enjoyed
ever afterwards.

On returning from his Caribbean cruise, Easton found
Harbour Grace in the hands of French Basques who had
captured his fort during his absence. The Basque fleet, led
by a ship named the *St. Malo*, sailed out to give battle. As
with all of Easton's engagements, we have no details of the
ensuing fight — only the results. The Basque ships were
sunk or captured, and the *St. Malo* herself was stranded on
a small islet near the entrance to Harbour Grace, subsequently known as Easton's Isle (later corrupted to "Eastern
Isle" and now to "Eastern Rock"). The pirates then landed
and recaptured their fort. They lost forty-seven men in the
battle, burying them at Bear Cove, just north of Harbour
Grace, in a place still known as "The Pirates' Graveyard."

They gutted, stripped, and burned the *San Sebastian* at
Ship's Head, Harbour Grace. A large anchor of Spanish
design was recovered there by Captain William Stevenson in
1885 — perhaps the only relic found from the treasure ship.

In 1612, while maintaining the fort at Harbour Grace,
Easton moved his personal headquarters to Ferryland and
there built "a great house" on a place called Fox Hill. This
harbour, later the headquarters of Sir David Kirke, had
obvious advantages. It was on the open ocean, near Cape

Race and major shipping routes. Its entrance was guarded by the steep and easily fortified Isle aux Bois. In all its long history, Ferryland was never successfully attacked by sea. A tiny inner harbour called "The Pool" could be used as a sort of dry dock. A steep hill called "The Gaze" rose above the beach and gave a wide view of the ocean in every direction.

Easton was now wealthy by any reasonable standards and willing to retire, so he began negotiating with King James for a pardon. Such pardons could be bought from the King if the price was right, as reported in the journal of Jean Chevalier of Jersey, a contemporary and friend of the pirates and a supporter of the Stuart monarchy. Chevalier names no figures but says English pirates paid "considerable sums of money" for their pardons.

Easton sent off at least three appeals for a pardon by three separate routes, one of them by Whitbourne, who agreed to take his letter to the Killigrews who in turn would become "humble petitioners to Your Majesty for his pardon." Whitbourne, as always, carried out his commission with dispatch: "And so, leaving Easton, I came for England, and gave notice of his intention, letting pass my voyage that I intended for Naples, and lost both my labour and charges: for before my arrival there was a pardon granted, and sent him from Ireland."

Guy, in fact, had earlier reported that Easton was sending a Captain Harvey in a ship to Ireland with his request for a pardon. But King James, obviously scenting gold, pardoned Easton *twice*. Both pardons are preserved in the British Public Records, the first dated February 1612, the second, November 1612.

The Public Records also has an estimate of Easton's

depredations in Newfoundland: from English ships, 100 cannons, victuals and munition to the value of 10,400 pounds, "besides 500 fishermen of His Majesty's subjects taken from their honest trade of fishing (many being volunteers) but the most enforced..."; from the French, 25 ships; from the Flemish, 1 "great ship"; from the Portuguese, 12 ships.

All this helped to keep the pirate corporation, with its thousands of employees, afloat, but the real wealth came from Easton's private war with Spain, which he continued vigorously even while waiting for the King's pardon. He must have known that the pardon had been issued even if, as Whitbourne suggests, he never actually received a piece of parchment with the royal seal. Whitbourne, indeed, was subtly chiding the King for his choice of messengers. Easton, he says, "was hovering with those ships and riches upon the coast of Barbary, as he promised, with a longing desire and full expectation to be called home," but "lost that hope by a too much delaying of time by him who carried the pardon." If only the King had sent one of his multiple pardons by Captain Whitbourne!

Judging by Easton's subsequent career, he couldn't have cared all that much about the King's pardon. He remained at Ferryland until he received word that the Spanish Plate Fleet was preparing to sail from the West Indies by way of the Azores for Spain. This was an annual convoy by which the Spanish transferred their loot from Central America to their home treasury. It was a complex operation that involved using donkey trains on the Isthmus of Panama, making up ships' cargoes under armed guard, and assembling a fleet, all of which took many weeks. Meanwhile, word from paid inform-ers could be passed to trading ships that in turn could sell their information to Spain's enemies. This form of betrayal had happened in the past, and now it happened once again.

Easton had boasted as early as 1612 that he would intercept the Spanish Plate Fleet. Now, in 1614, he did it. He sailed for the Azores with fourteen ships and deployed them in a wide arc to the south and west of the islands. Sure enough, the Spaniards sailed right into the ambush. Again, we have no details of the battle. We only know that Easton arrived off the Barbary Coast with four Spanish treasure ships containing the annual loot of an empire and was entertained as a conquering hero by the Bey of Tunis, who was said (with what truth no one can determine) to have offered him command of his fleet and a share in his kingdom.

In any case, the Great Easton remained for less than a year with the Moorish prince. By 1615 he had made a deal with the Duke of Savoy and had moved to Villefranche on the Riviera. There he purchased a palace, adopted the title Marquis of Savoy, and, in Whitbourne's phrase, "lived rich." Contemporary accounts estimate Easton's personal fortune at two million pounds sterling.

There is no way to translate this fortune accurately into contemporary terms — the values of too many things have changed. But a penny in Easton's time could buy many of the same things that a dollar can buy today (a dollar, originally, was exactly one fifth of a pound). So, in today's purchasing power it might be fair to say that Easton retired with a fortune in the neighbourhood of about five hundred million dollars.

He became Master of Ordnance for the Duke of Savoy, with whom he took part in at least one military campaign — an attack on the Duchy of Mantua, during which he "distinguished himself by the management and placement of his guns." After that, his career ends in silence.

But there is a monument to him at Harbour Grace, erected by the Government of Canada, with a bronze plaque giving a brief account of his career. Across Conception Bay from Harbour Grace lies the settlement of Kellegrews, named, at many years' remove, for members of the family who sponsored Easton in England. Around the shores of that bay where he fought the Basques, he is remembered in legend and admired as a leader of free spirits in an age of servitude. Did he set free the black slaves whom Captain Rashley was preparing to sell to the Spanish colonies? It would suit his legend if he had.

A town is named for the *Happy Adventure*, but it is only one of many Newfoundland places named for pirate ships. Others include Heart's Content, Heart's Desire, and Black Joke Cove.

In Conception Bay today there are hundreds of people with the surname "Easton." It is, actually, one of the commonest names in that part of Newfoundland. Did some of their ancestors, back in the seventeenth century, follow the old custom of adopting the name of a patron? It is certainly possible. No one knows for sure, but we are free to speculate that many of them may be descended from the "volunteers" whom Easton recruited into his crews — humble fishermen without surnames who followed him to his triumph over the Spanish fleet, took part in the share out of the wealth, then returned to the colony with money enough to become planters, adopting their captain's name in his honour.

CHAPTER 2
HENRY MAINWARING

W HILE EASTON WAS still at Ferryland preparing for his great venture against the Spanish Plate Fleet, Henry Mainwaring arrived, less like an avenging angel than a disciple following the master's steps. The Public Records for 1614 record the event:

> *Captain Maneringe with divers other captains arrived in Newfoundland the 4th of June having eight sails of warlike ships...from all the harbours whereof they commanded carpenters, maryners, victuals, munitions.... Of every six maryners they take one.... From the Portugal ships they took all their wine and other provisions save their bread; from a French ship in Harbour Grace they took*

*10,000 fish; some of the company of many ships
did run away unto them.... And so they departed
the 14th September having with them from the
fishing fleet about 400 maryners and fishermen,
many volunteers, many compelled.*

Mainwaring, somewhat more the aristocrat than Easton, always acted like one born to rule. The squadron he outfitted in 1612 to run down and capture Easton consisted of just three ships. Clearing from the Thames he made straight for Falmouth Bay near Land's End in Cornwall, where the Killigrews had their headquarters (their connection with the pirates being an open secret), and there learned that the quarry had flown.

This presented a problem. Mainwaring had almost certainly been backed by a corporation of aristocrats, fitting out three ships of war being a costly job, and had counted on laying claim to his share of Easton's loot. He called a conference of the ships' masters in his great cabin, and they agreed that since there was no prospect of catching pirates, the best way to make the expedition pay would be to go off after some Spaniards.

Unlike Easton, Mainwaring had direct access to Court. His family had been prominent in the Crusades and in the Wars of the Roses. Some of them were scholars and courtiers under Elizabeth I. He had been admitted to Oxford at the age of twelve, had his first degree at the age of fifteen, served briefly in the army, and was received at Court at the age of twenty-two.

Mainwaring applied to the King for an enlargement of his letters of marque to allow him to prey upon Spanish shipping. Though England was at peace with Spain, this commission was granted, with the stipulation that his acts of war must be confined to the western seas and not committed in European waters. But Mainwaring must have received assurance from the King or from Nottingham, the King's desk admiral, that any harassment of Spain would be viewed with tolerance, for he was hardly underway for the second time before he called his captains together and announced that they would capture Spanish ships whenever and wherever they had the chance.

Instead of heading west, they went south to Marmora on the Barbary Coast of Africa and began intercepting Spanish ships near the Strait of Gibraltar. While in North Africa, Mainwaring was received by the Bey of Tunis and was vastly impressed with Moorish civilization. In the Bey's dominions he could walk abroad without weapons by day or by night, for there were none of the thieves, footpads, pickpockets, and cutpurses that infested every city and town in England.

Since the North African Muslims were permanently at war with Spain, their harbours provided excellent bases from which pirates could prey on Spanish ships. Some seventeenth-century writers credit Easton and Mainwaring with teaching the Muslims their seamanship — hardly true, since the Barbary corsairs had centuries of seamanship behind them. What they did teach the Muslims was the superiority of the new sailing ship over the galleys and lateen-rigged luggers of the Mediterranean and the superiority of modern cannons over the bronze antiques still used by the Moorish princes. Mainwaring became a sort of admiral or captain-general of the port of Marmora and was able to offer protection to English shipping trading into Italy.

He also negotiated an English peace with Salee, then an independent sultanate famous for its own brand of pirates — the Salee Rovers. He secured from Salee the release of some hundreds of English prisoners held there as slaves, many of them serving in the galleys where they would have died without his intervention.

Mainwaring, despite his indiscretions, may never have fallen completely out of favour with King James. He consistently acted like an English ambassador at large. No warrant was ever issued against him from London, and it is to be noted that Whitbourne always spoke of him with respect. Nevertheless, he is listed in the English Public Records among the pirates and was certainly so regarded not only by the Spanish, French, and Portuguese, but also by English merchants and colonists.

Mainwaring's move to Newfoundland was prompted by the need for crewmen and for refitting his squadron, which had been on the move for two years. Of the eight ships that arrived with him, five probably belonged to independent pirate captains in temporary alliance under his leadership.

In an address to the King written several years later, he described Newfoundland as the best place in the world for outfitting pirate ships, as it had plentiful stores and munitions, ships' gear, maritime tradesmen of every sort, and experienced seamen *more than willing to join pirate crews as volunteers*. He flatly denied that he had "enforced" any of his men. On the contrary, his decision to allow only one man in six to volunteer was made so as not to interfere too severely with the proper employments of the fishery.

His arrival in Newfoundland was widely reported and discussed. His flagship, the *Princess*, caused a good deal of comment on her own account because she was perhaps unequalled by anything afloat for her combination of speed, handiness, and firepower.

Although she lacked the towering, top-heavy, castle-like look of the great Spanish ships, she had extra decks fore and aft, allowing her to mount extra guns in banks, one row above the other. Her three masts were rigged with square sails up to and including what were later called "royals," permitting more flexibility than either the merchant or warships of her time. She had a large fore-and-aft mainsail for tacking in close quarters and on her bowsprit a series of spritsails including a tiny spritsail topsail mounted at the very tip, nearly useless for speed but a neat little gadget for making very fast turns.

In fair weather the *Princess* was steered by a whipstaff — a long lever that went down through the upper deck to a pivot, then to an iron ring connected to the tiller, so that if you moved the whipstaff one way, the tiller moved the other. It provided extra leverage, but not enough to manage the ship in a storm. At such times she was steered with the aid of ropes running through pulleys to the tiller, several men to each rope. No one had yet thought of attaching the ropes to a wheel!

The *Princess* was fitted with cast-iron guns, the latest product of the gun foundries on the Sussex Wold. They had longer range, more accuracy, and could be reloaded and fired more rapidly than any other guns of the time. Some of them, test-fired at the foundries, could hit targets dead centre at ranges of half a mile or more. A few years later, such guns would revolutionize naval warfare. Mainwaring was also using a new tactic — the line of battle. His ships sailed in line and concentrated their fire, broadside, on a target. Perhaps Easton had used this technique before him. In any case, it was an invention of the English pirate admirals, soon to be adopted by the world's navies and employed for the next three hundred years.

Mainwaring's ship (he was absolutely in love with her) stood out like a flower among the drab fishing fleet. She was painted a dazzling sunshine yellow, with numerous brass fittings that he kept shining like gold. Moreover, real gold leaf was applied generously to scroll work at the bow and stern. She undoubtedly also had a gilded figurehead, although he never mentioned it in his writings — possibly a mermaid or a unicorn, both of which were popular at the time.

While in Newfoundland Mainwaring plundered French and Portuguese ships indiscriminately, probably without meeting the slightest resistance. The captains of these ships complained to their governments, and these, in turn, complained to King James, but there the matter ended — bills for damages were sometimes presented but were never paid. Mainwaring took over Easton's fort at Harbour Grace and may have built a careenage for cleaning and repairing ships. Like Easton, he entertained Captain Whitbourne and may have used him as a messenger to the King, although on precisely what mission Whitbourne prudently neglects to say: "He caused me to spend much time in his company, and from him I returned into England; although I was bound from thence to Marseilles, to make sale of such goods as I had, and other employments etc."

Mainwaring does not mention Whitbourne or any of his dealings with the government during the years of his "indiscretions," but he does say that the Bey of Tunis offered him command of his fleet, agreeing that he might remain a Christian and return to England whenever he chose. He did not accept this offer. Instead, with his newly recruited crews of Newfoundland fishermen he sailed back to Marmora and renewed his profitable war with Spain.

By now Mainwaring had become such a problem that the Spaniards fitted out a squadron of five warships especially to deal with him. They caught him off the coast of Portugal in the summer of 1615. According to his own account, the battle took place on "Mid-Summer's Day," but his descendant and biographer, G.E. Mainwaring, says it was in July. This probably means July 4, "Mid-Summer's Day" by the pre-Gregorian calendar, although twelve days after the solstice.

The battle lasted "throughout all the daylight hours." Mainwaring was outnumbered, but the Spanish ships were outsailed and outgunned. They still relied on the old tactic of sailing up to individual ships, hammering away at point-blank range, and then boarding them (using grappling hooks) for hand-to-hand combat. Mainwaring, with his superior guns and better sail plan, was able to stand off, perhaps completely out of range and certainly beyond the reach of accurate fire from the Spaniards, while raking their decks with repeated broadsides. When they realized that they were no match for the pirate, they fled into Lisbon harbour and took shelter under powerful shore batteries that Mainwaring could not approach. The arrival of the defeated Spanish squadron was observed by the Venetian ambassador, who sent home a gleeful report to his government.

Spain sued for peace. They sent an envoy to Villefranche, where Mainwaring had taken up temporary residence, and offered him twenty thousand gold ducats to enter the Spanish

naval service. But by now Mainwaring was hoping for a similar invitation from England, so he refused the Spanish offer,
adding that he did not need the help of the King of Spain to
secure twenty thousand pieces of Spanish gold.

The Spanish ambassador in London then obtained the
support of the French ambassador, and together they made
a presentation to King James, the substance of which was
that they would consider the tripartite peace between the
three governments to have been violated unless England
stopped Mainwaring or declared him an outlaw and issued
orders for his arrest.

So James, in turn, sent an envoy to Villefranche with the
offer of a pardon, an invitation to Court, and the promise
of a commission in the Royal Navy. Mainwaring accepted.
The pardon was issued under the Great Seal of England,
dated June 9, 1616. It included a general amnesty for all
the captains and crews serving in Mainwaring's squadron.
Mainwaring then returned to England bearing "a large sum
of money," which he presented to the King. Jean Chevalier,
who records the event and doubtless knew just how much
Mainwaring paid for his pardon, says no more than that.

The pardoned pirate was still under thirty years of age,
but had established himself as, with the possible exception
of Easton, the foremost seaman of his time. James gave him
a knighthood and the command of Dover Castle, England's
principal fortress on the North Sea. He was elected to
parliament from Dover and rose through a succession of
commands in the Royal Navy until he became a vice-admiral.

He now turned his mind to the suppression of piracy and
the safety of the seas. He wrote a short treatise on the origins
and suppression of piracy in which he had the gall to counsel

the King to desist from the policy of pardoning pirates. He also wrote a brief account of his own life and a manual of seamanship — *The Seaman's Dictionary* — which became the foundation of all subsequent seaman's manuals in English.

Under his influence the government began issuing commissions for the capture of pirates, making such captures financially rewarding by offering their holders forty percent of the "prize money" realized from the sale of ships and cargoes. Such a commission was issued to John Mason, the governor of the Colony at Cupids, Newfoundland, from 1616 to 1626 (and afterwards founder of New Hampshire). Mason, in turn, issued commissions to others and succeeded in taking a number of pirate prizes, among them the large and picturesquely named *Heart's Desire*.

By 1620 the government, under Mainwaring's influence, was not only commissioning privateers to take pirates as prizes, but was putting the ships of the Royal Navy back into service. By 1621 they ordered a mass impressment of sailors to man these ships. The action had the effect of setting off a new wave of piracy. Few men would serve voluntarily in the navy of the time, where they were herded about the decks by bo'suns with rope's-ends and officers with canes and hanged if they fought back. To escape impressment, many sailors who had served on trading and slaving ships shipped out to Newfoundland with the fishing fleet that year — far more than could find employment in the fishery. Most of these men turned pirate.

Through this policy Sir Henry Mainwaring encountered his most troublesome successor, John Nutt of Lympston, Devonshire. Nutt was no sooner in Newfoundland in the summer of 1621 than he formed a conspiracy with other refugees from the press gang to seize a French ship and fit her out as a pirate. They promptly captured two large trading vessels, one French and one English, and took their loot to Ferryland, where they were welcomed and entertained by the governor of the Ferryland colony, Sir George Calvert, who was almost certainly a broker for pirated goods.

Nutt and his companions plundered the Newfoundland fleets for the rest of that summer, then sailed back to England and set up as Channel pirates, using the Killigrews as intermediaries. The King issued a warrant for Nutt's arrest and at the same time, against Mainwaring's advice, let it be known that a pardon might be considered if the price was right. The Killigrews sent word back that Nutt was willing to discuss a deal, and Vice-Admiral Sir John Eliot went to negotiate with him.

Eliot and Nutt agreed to a price of five hundred pounds. Then Eliot tricked Nutt into going ashore without a safe-conduct and had him clapped into irons, planning to have him hanged and to seize his ship. But by this time Calvert (later Lord Baltimore, founder of Maryland) had returned to England and he intervened on Nutt's behalf. A payment for Nutt's release was agreed on (doubtless higher than the one Nutt had negotiated with Eliot), and Nutt promptly went off to Ireland where he collected a new fleet and began preying on shipping bound in and out of the Bristol Channel.

This time Mainwaring fitted out an armed squadron under Captain Plumleigh to arrest Nutt, but Plumleigh found the pirate in command of a fleet of twenty-seven ships and was lucky to escape without having his own ships taken as prizes. Nutt was never brought to justice. He retired wealthy and disappeared from history.

Mainwaring was the chief architect of the new Royal Navy under James I and remained actively involved when James was succeeded by Charles I. He fought for King Charles in the English Civil War, spending whatever fortune remained to him from his days as a pirate in the losing fight against Oliver Cromwell. His last military action was the defence of Pendennis Castle, the old stronghold of the Killigrews in Cornwall. There he withstood a five-month siege by the Roundheads after the rest of the country had capitulated.

But it was hopeless. In the end Mainwaring and some companions escaped to the Isle of Jersey, where they took refuge with Jean Chevalier, the royalist and diarist whose journals reveal some of the details of the intimate relationship between pirates and governments that were a feature of the Stuart dynasty.

Cromwell never did take the Channel Islands, but in 1651 Sir Henry Mainwaring petitioned for a pardon and for permission to return to England. He was almost destitute. His estate was valued at eight pounds, consisting only of a horse and some clothing. According to the public records, his fine was fixed at one-sixth of his estate and was paid on December 18, 1651, in the amount of one pound, six shillings, and eight pence.

Mainwaring died a year and a half later and was buried at St. Giles's Church, Camberwell, on May 15, 1653.

For some reason — perhaps because he was too much the aristocrat — Mainwaring never enjoyed the popularity that Easton did in Newfoundland, and there has never been any move to erect monuments to his memory. But in other respects his reputation has fared better than that of his older rival. G.E. Mainwaring went some way toward rescuing him from undeserved oblivion with his two-volume treatise, *The Life and Works of Sir Henry Mainwaring*, handsomely published by the Jersey Historical Society.

Mainwaring is often quoted by marine historians but is otherwise generally neglected. He lived in troubled times and had the misfortune to serve the Stuarts rather than the Tudors. Otherwise his name might well stand beside that of Sir Francis Drake as one of the true founders of Britain's rulership of the seas.

CHAPTER 3
DAVID KIRKE AND THE BAND OF BROTHERS

F EW OF THE GREAT ADVENTURERS of early
Canada led such flamboyant lives as the Kirkes. Five
brothers who sailed as captains of a privateering fleet,
they enjoyed careers that even Francis Drake or Walter
Raleigh might have envied. Three of them were knighted
by the King of England. One became governor of Quebec;
another, governor of Newfoundland. They cornered the
Canadian fur trade, made and lost fortunes, counted the
crowned heads of Europe among their friends and enemies,
and, when their other enterprises had reached the lowest
ebb, they founded a fishing colony at Ferryland.

The Kirke brothers were born at Dieppe, on the French
side of the English Channel. The name is spelled "Kirq"

in French documents of the seventeenth century. But the channel ports had been disputed territory for hundreds of years, and the Kirkes may always have regarded themselves as subjects of the English king. In any case, England was the country they served, and all their commercial ties were with London. David Kirke, the eldest, was the unquestioned leader of the clan. Serving with him were his brothers Lewis, Thomas, John, and James, all soldiers of fortune in an age when it was still possible to own a private navy and to conquer and rule a country on behalf of a corporation of merchants. That, among many other things, is just what they did.

Sometime around 1625 the Kirkes hatched a bold plan to capture the Canadian fur trade, which was then mainly in the hands of a French monopoly centred in Quebec and Acadia (New Brunswick and Nova Scotia). A series of monopolies had been granted by the King of France, though never enforced with complete success. The Kirkes' chance came in 1627, when, after a relatively long peace, Britain and France were at war over the question of the rights of French Protestants. David Kirke and his brothers secured letters of marque from King Charles I of England, authorizing them to annoy the King's enemies, and they formed a company to outfit and provision a squadron for an attack on New France. One of their backers was the young Duke of Hamilton, who was in line to succeed to the throne of Scotland after Charles's own family, and was a trusted councillor of the King's.

Six years earlier Charles's father, James I, had made a grant to another Scottish nobleman, Sir William Alexander, giving him title to what are now the provinces of Nova

Scotia and New Brunswick. The territory was then occupied by the French, and James was not at war with France, but following the policy of his predecessor Elizabeth I, he always took the attitude that you could have peace in Europe while privateering and piracy continued with official blessing in the New World.

So when the five Kirkes, in five strongly armed ships, set out to seize the fur trade from the French, the first place they steered for was New Scotland, as the English had begun to call it. Besides their privateering crews, they carried a few Scottish colonists who had their own ideas about fur trading and a willingness to set up and defend forts in Sir William Alexander's domain, once the Kirkes had made it safe for occupation. The arrival of a Scottish governor (Alexander's son) and a Scottish colony was made easy by the fact that Acadia was undefended and the few French peasants who lived there were content to accept any government that would allow them to get on with their own lives.

The ships in which David Kirke and his brothers sailed from England in 1628 were an improvement over the floating castles that the Spaniards had used in their futile attempt to invade England forty years earlier — handier, more seaworthy, lower in the water — but still clumsy and slow compared with the ships that were to come later in the "golden age of sail." All five ships seem to have been large and well armed: three-masted, carrying at least one full course of guns on each side, perhaps ten to twenty to a broadside. Apart from this, their great strength consisted in the fact that each was fitted out for warfare, with crews of eighty men or more, compared with the twenty to thirty sailors manning the merchant ships of the time.

The mainmast, carrying three courses of square sails, was stepped somewhat aft of amidships; the foremast, next in importance, with either two or three courses, was near the bow. The third mast, at the stern, carried a lateen sail as well as a square sail. This helped the ship to steer and run a little closer to the wind than a ship with all square sails. Headsails — jibs rigged to the bowsprit — helped the ship to manoeuvre, but in even the best ships of the time the bowsprit might also be made to carry a spritsail topsail — a square sail on a kind of miniature mast projecting upward from the tip of the bowsprit. This awkward-looking rig could be used to help tack the ship, to bring the bow around in a hurry. In addition to their sails the two principal masts would also carry fighting tops — railed platforms high above the deck, from which a seaman could hurl pots of burning pitch or canisters filled with gunpowder and scrap iron onto the enemy deck. There were also galleries built around the stern-railed walkways that could be manned by pikemen and musketmen to help fend off boarders.

The ship's wheel for steering had not yet been invented. Instead the rudder was controlled by a whipstaff, a long lever connected to the tiller, so that moving the whipstaff one way moved the tiller the other. In heavy weather the ship was kept on course by ropes rigged to the rudder and run through pulleys, with three or four men on either side to haul or slack away as ordered by the sailing master. With the help of sails trimmed for steering, it was not as awkward as it sounds, but the wheel, when it finally forced itself upon the attention of ship designers, provided a great mechanical advantage, allowing one man to do the work of two or three, controlling even a large ship in heavy weather.

David Kirke, a seaman ahead of his time, may have fought his ships "in line of battle" when the occasion arose. In this manoeuvre the ships of a squadron sailed a single course, close together, allowing them to concentrate their fire on a target. It was a simple, effective tactic invented by the pirate squadrons of the early seventeenth century to multiply the effect of a broadside by the number of ships firing. But such is the conservatism of the professional military mind that the navies of Europe did not adopt it until 1650 or later (probably under the influence of Sir Henry Mainwaring, who was privateersman, pirate, and admiral, in turn).

Kirke had the advantage of a strong personality, unquestioned leadership, and the full loyalty of the four captains, his brothers, all of whom were members of the privateering corporation and seeking their family fortune together. A pirate at heart, a born commander, with five well-found fighting machines in his squadron, Kirke also had great fortune that first year in North America.

He sailed first to the southern tip of Nova Scotia, where he captured and burnt a number of small French trading posts, among them Miscou and Chebouge, just south of the inlet where the town of Yarmouth now stands. Having "annoyed" the enemy in Acadia most effectively, the Kirkes circled back through the Strait of Canso and headed up the St. Lawrence to Tadoussac, the post at the mouth of the Saguenay River, which had been a centre of the fur trade long before Quebec was founded and continued as a centre of fur trading, walrus hunting, and whale hunting long afterwards. Despite its importance Tadoussac was not heavily fortified. The French fur monopolies had never managed to get more than a few dozen colonists to go out to Canada at any one time, and on the St. Lawrence they had concentrated all their efforts at Quebec. Tadoussac, which received furs coming down from the region of Hudson Bay, was a way station, occupied by a few middlemen in the fur trade, most of them Basque fishing captains. The Kirkes took it over almost without firing a shot and transferred a year's supply of furs to their holds. A nice beginning. Even better was to follow.

This was the point where luck played straight into David Kirke's hands. He had expected three or four supply ships to call at Tadoussac on their way upriver to Quebec. They always stopped there to take on local pilots before continuing to the French capital, where Samuel de Champlain held sway, collecting furs from canoe routes running into the heart of the continent. But instead of three or four ships, no fewer than eighteen French vessels sailed into the trap. It was the year of the great colonizing fleet fitted out by the Company of the Hundred Associates of New France, intended to launch Canada on a new era of farming as well as fur trading. The ships were armed merchantmen, and the colonists included a few soldiers sent to reinforce Champlain's precarious hold on the St. Lawrence, always threatened as it was by the powerful aboriginal confederacy of the Iroquois. But the French ships were not fitted out for naval warfare; they had expected, at the worst, to have to deal with a lone pirate or two, and the Kirke brothers rounded them up like sheep. One ship escaped upriver in the fog, but the other seventeen were taken into Tadoussac as prizes and later shepherded home to England in triumph. This coup not only paid all the expenses of the expedition several times over but left Champlain's colony at Quebec in a state bordering on starvation. It survived the winter on roots and berries and what food it could get from neighbouring Montagnais hunters.

Among the shiploads of prisoners that David Kirke took home with him that year for eventual repatriation to France was Claude La Tour, a colonist and fur trader who had been among the early settlers at Port Royal and whose son Charles owned trading posts at Cape Sable and LaHave on Nova Scotia's Atlantic shore. Somehow, Kirke seems to have missed those small forts. By the time they reached England, Kirke had persuaded La Tour to refuse patriation and to enter the service of the King of England. New France, he assured La Tour, was finished. Henceforth North America would be an English continent.

Charles I was especially grateful to Kirke's company, because the Crown's share of the loot helped to rescue his treasury from bankruptcy. The King gave Kirke a knighthood and received him at Court. La Tour too must have been received by the King, because he not only entered the services of Sir William Alexander's colonizing company but also married one of the ladies-in-waiting to the Queen. Alexander was already Secretary for Scotland and Lieutenant Governor of Nova Scotia. A year or so later he would become the Viscount Stirling and eventually Earl of Donovan. He made a large grant of land to La Tour on the Atlantic coast of Nova Scotia, including the trading posts at Cape Sable and LaHave, occupied by La Tour's son, and created him a knight-baronet of New Scotland.

In the spring of 1629 Sir David Kirke took his privateering fleet back to Canada, landed Alexander's colonists at several posts, most of them, including Sir Claude La Tour and his wife, at Port Royal, then sailed off to complete his conquest of New France. Except for small-time farmers raising grain and pasturing sheep and cattle around the shores of the Annapolis Basin, the French had abandoned Port Royal. The fort had long since been destroyed. So the Scottish settlers built a new fort at a place now called Granville Beach, where it remained in various states of disrepair for the next two hundred years under the name of the Scotch Fort, though the Scots remained there for only three years.

While this was going on, La Tour headed off to his own domain on the Atlantic coast to enlist his son Charles in the service of England. Much to his astonishment Charles refused. The elder La Tour then brought a party of armed men to Cape Sable and tried to take the post by force, but Charles defended his little fort at gunpoint and drove his father back to Port Royal. So Claude La Tour never did occupy the lands granted to him by Alexander, and his son was later able to claim that he had always remained loyal to the King of France.

Meanwhile Kirke's fleet had sailed back to Tadoussac and transferred to its holds another year's supply of furs. At Tadoussac they had the good luck to meet Étienne Brûlé, a man who had spent twenty years among the aboriginals, spoke their languages, and knew the country better than anyone alive. Brûlé had been in Canada from the age of fourteen and had no wish to live anywhere else. He believed that New France was finished and had no intention of being shipped back to Europe in a prisoner exchange. Like La Tour, he entered the British service and piloted the privateers upriver until they could anchor just out of cannon shot of Champlain's fort on the headland of Quebec.

Kirke sent a message to Champlain under flag of truce, demanding his surrender. And the governor of New France, having neither powder, shot, nor even food to sustain a siege, surrendered on honourable terms for repatriation to France. The few soldiers at the fort surrendered with him and were repatriated. The handful of colonists who operated tiny farms in the area remained and, like Brule and La Tour, agreed to serve the English.

Sir Lewis (also called Louis) Kirke remained at Quebec as governor and collected boatloads of furs from the Huron and Montagnais traders, as Champlain had done. Other ships of the squadron returned to Tadoussac and continued to monopolize the furs from the northern aboriginals. The Kirkes thus achieved a total monopoly of the fur trade of Canada, something that no company before their time had ever managed to do.

In the words of one historian, the Kirkes "reaped a fortune in furs." Perhaps. It is true that they monopolized the fur trade for at least five years, perhaps six. But they were not acting entirely on their own behalf. They were agents of a wealthy cabal of London merchants, including powerful members of the Court, and those merchants may well have reaped most of the fortune, though they later accused Sir David Kirke of embezzling some of the company's profits.

Except for Charles La Tour, hovering as a kind of outlaw on the extreme southern tip of Nova Scotia, New France was now entirely in English hands, its conquest complete. The Newfoundland historian D.W. Prowse described the virtually bloodless conquest as the most brilliant naval exploit in colonial history. But then, in March 1632, at the Treaty of St. Germainen-Laye, King Charles I returned all of Kirke's conquests to the King of France. Inexplicable? A policy of scuttle, as Prowse called it? Not at all. Charles was on the brink of bankruptcy once again, and he sold New France back to the French for a payment disguised as the dowry of his wife, the French Princess Henrietta Maria. Even before the treaty was signed, the King had already ordered the Scots colonists out of Nova Scotia. So the chief beneficiary of Sir David Kirke's conquests was the King's treasury. But treaty or no treaty the Kirkes continued to hold Quebec and Tadoussac for another year and so picked up another year's lucrative supply of furs.

As a reward for their services, Sir David Kirke and his company, which now included not only the Duke of Hamilton but also the Earls of Pembroke and Holland, received a grant from Charles I giving them title to the whole island of Newfoundland. Like his father, Charles distributed his royal grants with a free hand. Included in the territory of which Kirke now became governor was a colony founded at Ferryland by Sir George Calvert, Lord Baltimore, also under royal grant. Baltimore had left Newfoundland, as the King's grant noted, but many of his colonists were still there, including an appointed governor, and there were other planters in other harbours. Kirke now made Ferryland his capital and expelled the Baltimore colonists by force, bringing out a hundred colonists of his own. He enforced the payment of rents by colonists in other harbours, some of them established there long before his arrival, and collected taxes at gunpoint from foreign fishing ships. This last exaction brought screams of protest from the French ambassador in London, who claimed, quite truthfully, that his nation had fished in those waters by ancient right. Kirke also issued licences for taverns — indeed he seems to have treated the rum trade as his private monopoly. All this, especially his treatment of Baltimore's colonists, coupled with charges of embezzlement by his sponsors, brought on a complex series of lawsuits that continued for the rest of his life.

Meanwhile in Acadia the King of France had appointed the formidable Charles La Tour lieutenant general. La Tour's father and his father's wife had returned to the son's fold at Cape Sable, and all but two of the Scottish colonists had sailed for home. The two who remained married Acadian wives and entered La Tour's service. All very well, except that the King of France appointed another lieutenant general named Charles de Menou d'Aulnay, whose territory overlapped La Tour's and whose character was that of a medieval robber baron. The two lieutenant generals soon took to raiding each other's trading posts, killing each other's servants, and fitting out private navies to make war on each other.

Charles La Tour at first tried to get Sir David Kirke's assistance. He sailed to Ferryland, where Kirke received him amicably enough. What he promised Kirke heaven only knows, but it wasn't sufficient. Kirke by now was a personal friend of the King of England, and it would have taken more than La Tour could offer to make him disobey the King's orders to leave Nova Scotia to the French. La Tour then turned to Massachusetts, a colony that had earlier shown a lively and predatory interest in Acadia. The governor, like Kirke, refused to intervene personally against the orders of his King, but he allowed La Tour to purchase and outfit a squadron of private warships in Boston and to enlist men from Massachusetts as mercenaries.

Profits from the fur trade in the seventeenth century must have been enormous because Charles La Tour, who had no other resources than fur trading, fitted out four ships, armed them with thirty-eight cannons, and hired crews and fifty mercenaries, all at his own expense. He then sailed against d'Aulnay, who was hovering around the mouth of the St. John River in what is now New Brunswick, trying to capture a small fort that had been built there by La Tour. At La Tour's approach d'Aulnay fled, but La Tour pursued him across the Bay of Fundy and into the Annapolis Basin, finally cornering him at the Lequille River, near the place where Fort Anne and the town of Annapolis Royal were later built. Here there was a brief battle from which d'Aulnay fled, defeated. Soon afterwards he sailed to France for reinforcements and a fresh commission from the King.

The next year he returned, loaded with guns and parchments, styling himself "governor and lieutenant general for the King of France in all the coasts of Acadie." Once again he attacked La Tour's fort on the St. John River. La Tour was away at Cape Sable or one of his other posts and had left the fort in charge of his wife, Françoise Marie Jacquelin. She resisted the siege for three days, then surrendered under flag of truce on condition that she and all those inside would be given safe conduct. D'Aulnay then committed the blackest act of treachery in the history of New France. He seized all the men at gunpoint, offered one of them his life on condition that he act as hangman, and had all the others strung up, one by one, to the rafters of the fort, forcing Madame La Tour to watch the massacre, with a rope around her own neck. He didn't hang her, but within three weeks she too was dead, though apparently not from ill treatment.

La Tour fled first to Boston, then to Quebec. Meanwhile d'Aulnay enjoyed a monopoly in Acadia — but not for long. While travelling by canoe, he was drowned at the narrows that connects the Annapolis Basin and the French Basin, in the tide race where the causeway and tidal power station now stand. Tradition says that d'Aulnay was travelling with an aboriginal whom he had brutally abused some months earlier and that the drowning was no accident. Maybe. In any case Charles La Tour returned, with the renewed title of lieutenant general, and not only took over d'Aulnay's forts but even married d'Aulnay's widow, a woman who, like his former wife, possessed great strength of character and resolution and knew how to help her husband in time of battle.

Despite a charge of treason a few years earlier when he had hired English colonists to fight on his behalf, La Tour was described in his new letters patent as having "faithfully served the Kings of France for a period of forty-three years." This old freebooter, who ranged up and down Canada with musket and cannon for more than half a century, serving the French when they were in control and the English when they reconquered Acadia, finally died in his bed at the age of seventy-two in his home on the St. John River.

Sir David Kirke, the other great privateer whose career was so entwined with La Tour's, remained at Ferryland through turbulence and controversy, even when his partners in the privateering and trading company replaced him temporarily with another governor. When civil war broke out in England and the cause of the Royalists became hopeless, he offered King Charles I sanctuary at Ferryland, which he hoped to be able to defend with his own ships. He probably could have done it too, because when it was properly fortified, Ferryland was virtually unassailable by sea, but the King preferred to remain in England and face execution rather than desert his throne. A few months before he went to the scaffold he wrote Kirke, imploring him to find asylum for his sister, Lady Hawkins.

Kirke eventually made his peace with Cromwell, and his brother Sir James Kirke even managed to save the company by taking Cromwell's son-in-law into partnership. Brother John remained in London as the company's agent, but when he enlisted four hundred seamen to be sent out to Newfoundland as colonists, Cromwell's government refused to allow them to sail, believing that they were intended to help man a Royalist fleet, still at sea under *Prince Rupert.*

Eventually Sir David Kirke was recalled to London to face charges brought against him by the heirs of Lord Baltimore — a controversy that was never settled. He died in London, with the suit unresolved, but his wife and sons and grandsons all remained at Ferryland, where they established a large fishing enterprise. Lady Kirke, with her sons George, David, and Philip, owned fourteen boats manned by sixty-six fishermen in 1673, when the Dutch privateering fleet under Captain Jacob Everson attacked Ferryland and sacked the town. But even then the Kirkes stayed on and tried to rebuild their fortune. They were not finally dislodged from Ferryland until Pierre Le Moyne d'Iberville destroyed the English colonies in his great raid of 1696.

CHAPTER 4
SAILING AGAINST ACADIA

THE ANNAPOLIS BASIN, on the south shore of the Bay of Fundy, was regarded from the day of its discovery by French explorers as one of the most desirable places on the Atlantic coast. Champlain and Lescarbot both commented on its beauty and fruitfulness. Even today, people from many parts of North America live there by choice. A region coveted by both French and English settlers, perhaps its great desirability is one of the reasons it was subjected to so much murder, rape, and arson in its early years.

In 1613 a privateering raid from Virginia, commanded by Captain Samuel Argall, burned the undefended fort at Port Royal and destroyed all official marks of French occupation, using picks and chisels to efface the names of French captains and the fleur-de-lis emblems from a massive stone where they had been engraved. Between the Argall raid and the final British conquest of 1710 this area was fought over by rival fur-trading gangs and captured and sacked no fewer than five times by privateering fleets from the New England colonies to the south. The privateers usually headed for Port Royal, the Acadian capital, but they also attacked the undefended farming settlements at Minas and Chignecto, near the head of the Bay of Fundy, and the posts on the St. John River as far inland as Jemseg, a fur-trading station nearly fifty miles upstream from Reversing Falls, where the Fundy tides flow in and out of the St. John. There were other raids later, as we shall see, but none so vicious as those conducted by gangs of drunken looters from the waterfronts of Boston and other New England ports during the last half-century of the French regime in Acadia.

A force of some three hundred men landed at Port Royal in 1654, at a time when the little settlement was virtually undefended because England and France were temporarily at peace. Cromwell was ruling England at the time, and his ships, sent to attack New York (then held by the Dutch and called New Amsterdam), supported the raid, carried out mainly by New Englanders. The attack is hard to classify: piracy? undeclared war? privateering? It was certainly done on Cromwell's orders, though the orders were given secretly, and many of those involved were civilians. They captured the small coastal forts, then sailed into the Annapolis Basin, fought a brief battle with the defenders, deported the handful of French troops found there, and allowed the Acadian families to keep their farms. The raid was motivated partly by religion: "rooting out the Papists," but only the *ruling* Papists. The peasants were allowed to keep their religion as well as their hard-won farms on the reclaimed salt marshes.

Charles La Tour, who always managed to be a Huguenot when dealing with the English and a loyal son of the Church when dealing with the Most Catholic King of France, put on his Protestant hat, resurrected his father's title as knight-baronet of New Scotland, and, in partnership with two wealthy Englishmen, received from Cromwell's government a grant to most of what had been Acadia. One of his partners, Thomas Temple, was named governor, and he is generally regarded by historians as the first English governor of Nova Scotia, even though he was essentially a merchant, with his headquarters in Boston, and paid only brief visits to New Scotland. The whole story of allegiances in this era is bizarre: La Tour switched his nationality from French to English several times and his religion along with it; the Kirkes managed to serve both King Charles I and his archenemy Oliver Cromwell; and Temple, nominated by Cromwell as governor of Nova Scotia, also had a commission from King Charles II, then living in exile in France. After Cromwell's death and the King's return to England, Temple was created a knight-baronet of Nova Scotia.

Nevertheless, thirteen years after the English had captured Acadia, Charles II, who was deeply indebted to the King of France, signed a treaty returning it to France. The residents of the Boston colonies never really accepted this and neither did Temple. He managed to keep his company in control until 1670, three years after the treaty, but finally surrendered the province to the French.

However, the return of a French governor did not end privateering raids against Acadia. The same Dutch privateering fleet that sacked Ferryland in 1673 and assisted in the capture of New York also captured the French forts in Nova Scotia and New Brunswick, took the French governor of Acadia prisoner, and seized control of the fur trade. And speaking of divided loyalties, this same fleet, which had expelled the English from New York, landed its French prisoners at Boston, where the Acadian governor was held for ransom until Governor Frontenac of Quebec paid one thousand beaver skins.

All this occurred while England and France were at peace. But the excuse of another war, if any such excuse were needed, soon stirred the Boston merchants to yet another attack. John Nelson, nephew of Thomas Temple, was a prosperous merchant at Boston, and in 1690, shortly after the beginning of "King William's War" against the French, he approached the governor of Massachusetts, offering to outfit a privateering fleet at his own expense and capture Acadia, provided he could keep the plunder and enjoy the same monopoly of the fur trade that his uncle had enjoyed a generation earlier.

But the governor had other plans. He agreed that Massachusetts should grab Acadia, but instead of passing it over to Nelson, he invited a corporation of merchants to underwrite the enterprise and placed it in charge of Sir William Phips, an illiterate New England treasure hunter, who a few years before had recovered a fortune from the sea bottom and helped rescue the Stuart monarchy from the brink of bankruptcy. He had been rewarded with a knighthood and a modest share of the treasure.

When Phips failed to raise the seven hundred volunteers he figured would be needed to conquer Acadia, the governor authorized him to use press gangs, and he made the rounds of the taverns, grabbing whatever men he could find to fill his ships. He anchored his fleet of seven armed vessels off Port Royal on May 11, 1690. Faced by overwhelming odds, the French governor surrendered on terms that his garrison of eighty-five men could keep their arms and return to France and on condition that the Acadian farmers would not be molested. Phips treacherously violated the terms of surrender and turned his shiploads of ruffians loose in an orgy of looting. They destroyed the fort, attacked the church, pulled down the altar, chopped down the crucifix, and smashed the statues. So much for popery. They plundered every farm and private house they could reach in a two-day rampage, then sailed back to Boston with their prisoners. The Boston merchants were so pleased with Phips that they made him governor the following year.

About a month after this attack on Port Royal two shiploads of privateers from New York arrived in the Annapolis Basin. Furious at finding nothing left worth looting, they turned to murder, rape, and arson. They set fire to the remaining buildings, burned one family alive inside their house, and hanged two Acadian peasants whom they managed to catch. Then they sailed across the Bay of Fundy and attacked the post on the St. John River at Jemseg, where the interim governor of Acadia, Joseph Robineau de Villebon, had taken refuge. He was upriver with a party of aboriginals when they arrived and captured his fort. On his return he organized a counter-attack and drove the killers downriver, but they escaped with his ship as a prize and left him stranded.

He then journeyed up the St. John River by canoe to its junction with the Madawaska, up the Madawaska, over the height of land, and up the St. Lawrence to Quebec, arriving in time to help defend the capital of New France from capture by a fleet organized and led by Phips.

Meanwhile the Acadian peasants who had escaped up the Lequille River, as the Annapolis River was then called, came back to the Port Royal area and began rebuilding. The next year the French returned, installed Villebon as permanent governor, and sent two privateer vessels from Port Royal to harass the coast of New England.

The greatest privateer captain of that war — perhaps the greatest in the entire history of New France — sailed out of Placentia, the French fortress on the south coast of Newfoundland, in the years 1689 to 1694. He was John Svigaricipi, a Basque captain with a talent for naval warfare and a strong, fast ship, very able in pursuit and attack. Svigaricipi was credited with taking "hundreds" of English and colonial ships, most of them probably mere fishing vessels. His most outstanding feat was making a prize of a full British warship, the one-hundred-gun *Princess*, an action for which he was decorated by King Louis XIV. Unfortunately we have no details of the battles fought by this brilliant sea rover, just the barest outline of his career and a gravestone preserved in a museum at Placentia, where he was buried in 1694 after being killed at sea, apparently in the attack on Ferryland carried out by French privateers that year. The attack was a failure. The Ferryland fishing masters had taken guns from their ships and erected fortifications on the Isle aux Bois, making it impossible for the French squadron to force its way into the harbour. In a letter to the governor of Massachusetts, who offered them assistance, those independent fishing captains reported that they had fought off "the King's enemies" on two occasions by their own unaided efforts and were prepared to do the same again. However, they were obliterated by an overland attack in 1696, when Pierre Le Moyne d'Iberville led a force of French Canadians and Abenaki people from Placentia, capturing and burning every English settlement on the Avalon Peninsula, except for Carbonear Island, where the settlers successfully withstood a siege.

Peace returned in 1697, and all territories were restored to their pre-war owners. But four years later England and France were at it again in the War of the Spanish Succession (Queen Anne's War), which lasted thirteen years and put the final seal of doom on the Acadian colony. Near the beginning of the war the governor of New France made an extraordinary offer to the governor of Massachusetts, suggesting that the two colonies enter into a pact of neutrality, despite the impending war in Europe. Governor Bruillon of Acadia made a similar offer. But Governor Thomas Dudley of Massachusetts rejected the idea out of hand — and brought on his people a series of terrible raids by French Canadians and their aboriginal allies, including the far-famed Deerfield massacre in which fifty or more people were killed and more than a hundred taken prisoner. (Then, as in the future, any defeat by aboriginals, even of regular army units, was invariably labelled a "massacre.")

Dudley called in the Boston merchants and urged them to equip a fleet of privateers to prey on Acadia and any other parts of New France that they could reach. But especially Acadia. They began ranging north into the Bay of Fundy.

By the end of 1702 they had destroyed the French fishery in Nova Scotia (though not in the Gulf of St. Lawrence or Newfoundland) and had brought fourteen ships into Boston as prizes. In response the French stationed privateers at Port Royal and sailed them against English colonial shipping from Maine to New York, making a great nuisance of themselves, especially along the coast of Massachusetts.

By 1704 Massachusetts was organizing a great expedition to wipe out "that nest of pirates" at Port Royal. At the same time the government of Massachusetts offered a bounty of £100 each for the scalps of any aboriginals over ten years of age. One hundred pounds was enough to buy an adult slave or an excellent team of horses. The privateers did, in fact, return with scalps, though how many isn't clear — perhaps a dozen or so.

The naval force raised by the Boston merchants consisted of three warships with eighty-six guns, an armed shallop, thirty-six whaleboats, and fourteen transports with 550 men. They also carried a great store of rum and in the course of the raid captured French stores of brandy and wine, putting it all to such good use that most of the raiders were roaring drunk for a good part of the month and a half the raid lasted.

This was the famous expedition led by Benjamin Church, the New England Daniel Boone who had made his reputation fighting and capturing aboriginals and selling them into slavery by the hundreds, mostly to sugar plantations in the West Indies, where they lasted an average of five years before being worked and beaten to death. Church should have been able to take Port Royal with ease, perhaps even Placentia, and end French power on the Atlantic coast. But he didn't even make the attempt. Instead he raided isolated farming communities at Minas and Chignecto, slaughtered cattle, burned houses, barns, and churches, and broke down the dykes to allow the sea to flood the reclaimed crop lands. The whole fleet then gathered at Port Royal and demanded the surrender of the fort. The governor, with 193 men under his command, refused. Church, better at kidnapping aboriginals than capturing forts, sailed away without firing a shot, returned to Boston with his pitiful string of scalps from aboriginals over the age of ten, and was received as a conquering hero. But the raid is remembered in Nova Scotia for the sheer vandalism of Church's drunken crews.

By now Port Royal was expanding its privateering fleet, becoming the base for a company of French captains who ranged between Acadia and the French West Indies. That was more than the Boston merchants could endure, so in 1707 they organized an even greater fleet than the last, manned by more than thirteen hundred New Englanders (most of them shanghaied by press gangs) to confront the strengthened forces at Port Royal, where 185 French regulars, sixty Canadian militiamen, and ninety aboriginals awaited their coming. The New England forces besieged the fort for ten days and actually tried to carry it by storm under cover of darkness, but the French made deadly sallies out of the fort and laid ambushes for the attackers. When the New Englanders finally sailed away defeated, they left behind nearly a hundred dead.

Massachusetts wasn't prepared to give up so easily. The governor raised another hundred men and sent them off as reinforcements for the expedition. Two months after the first siege they were back in the Annapolis Basin once more. This time they again besieged the fort for ten days and fought valiantly against the French sallies, but in the end they retreated to their ships and sailed back to Boston having accomplished precisely nothing.

The garrison at Port Royal was now almost literally on its uppers, the men half-starved and only half-clothed. They had received no supplies from France in more than three years, but they managed to survive another two years and even fed five hundred prisoners who were housed there temporarily. Their supplies came from the privateers, who managed to capture enough food, clothing, guns, and ammunition from Yankee ships to keep the little French capital alive.

Finally, in 1710, a combined British and colonial force of thirty-five hundred men in thirty-six ships sailed against Port Royal and received the surrender on honourable terms of its 156 surviving defenders. Perhaps because the British were in charge, the terms were honoured, and the little garrison was allowed to march out carrying its flag and guns, dressed in whatever rags of uniforms it still possessed. Rarely in the history of human conflict had so little been achieved by so many against so few.

CHAPTER 5
JOHN PHILLIPS

A TYPICAL EIGHTEENTH-CENTURY desper-
ado, John Phillips began his pirate career in
Newfoundland and ended it less than a year later
off the coast of Massachusetts with an axe through the middle
of his skull. But his short career was violent, bloody, and well-
documented because, although he didn't live to be hanged,
some of his companions did, and the full story came out at
their trial. The complete transcript is preserved in the public
archives of the State of Massachusetts, and various related
documents are in the maritime museum at Boston.

The greatest days of piracy in eastern Canada were
between 1610 and the French military occupation of 1662,
when the great port of Placentia was fortified and garrisoned.

Those were the days of the pirate admirals when gentlemen of good family (and some not so good) commanded whole fleets and dealt with kings on almost equal terms.

A full century later, after the French power had been shattered by the War of the Spanish Succession, there was another great upsurge of piracy in the western and eastern Atlantic — this time by a new breed of brigands. No longer commanders of private navies like those of Ango, Raleigh, Easton, and Mainwaring, they were mostly men of low birth and little education, who learned to sail ships by rule of thumb and to capture unarmed merchant vessels while avoiding encounters with warships, which in those days were heavily gunned but rarely built for speed or for pursuit among islands in shallow waters.

This second period of piracy is often called the "Golden Age," not because there were more pirates or more successful ones than in earlier times, but because Daniel Defoe, the author of *Robinson Crusoe*, was on hand to document and romanticize their careers. Defoe wrote a book on the pirates of his times, undoubtedly compiled from interviews with men who had sailed on the ships of the major pirate captains. It became a bestseller and ran through many editions, making household words of such names as Blackbeard, Anne Bonny, and Edward Low, and giving the false impression that these were among the most successful pirates in history. There was no Defoe on hand to popularize the lives of such vastly more successful pirates as Easton and Mainwaring.

Phillips arrived in Canada when the Golden Age was all aglitter with doubloons and pieces of eight. He started life as an honest enough lad. Born into a family of English shipwrights, he decided in 1720 to emigrate to Newfoundland where there were opportunities in his trade because the English had taken over the shipyards at Placentia from the French under the treaty of 1713 and were operating a flourishing shipbuilding industry in their oldest colony.

The vessel on which John Phillips was travelling to Newfoundland was captured by a pirate as it came in over the Banks, and the young man was impressed into the pirate crew as ship's carpenter. As it happened, Phillips had fallen foul of one of the most blackhearted villains in the history of the sea, a sadistic cutthroat named Anstis who committed all the crimes of which pirates are usually accused.

Anstis fought without quarter, tortured any prisoners who fell alive into his hands, then flung them to the sharks. Captured women were gang-raped and murdered. The Anstis gang seemed really to be at war with the human race.

After some months of this, the company of thieves and butchers among whom Phillips had fallen decided to call it quits and seek a pardon, signing a round-robin petition for this purpose. Pirates of the Golden Age often retired in this way with a modest share of loot — a few hundred pounds a man, perhaps. Pardons were often freely granted in an effort to secure experienced seamen for the merchant fleets — if you couldn't get a pardon from one government, you could often get it from another, along with a change of citizenship.

The pardon was granted by Great Britain, and Phillips found honest work on a trading ship bound for England. There he transferred to another ship outward bound to Newfoundland and finally arrived at Placentia in the spring of 1723, three years after he had first set out for the colonies.

He failed to find work as a shipwright and went on to St. Pierre (then called St. Peter's Harbour because it was in English hands and not to be confused with St. Peters in Cape Breton Island which was still in the hands of the French). Here again no men of his trade were needed, and he was forced to sign on as servant in a fishing crew. He found this work so irksome and unrewarding that he began enquiring whether any of his fellow fishing servants would be interested in going on the account with him.

In those days many fisherman signed on for a season at almost no wages, while others served under indenture as virtual slaves. Even free men like Phillips were expected to work eighteen hours a day for little more than room, board, and a ration of rum. Food and rum were charged against their annual wages so that at the end of the fishing season they might get less than the cost of their passage home. In the circumstances he had little trouble finding sixteen men who agreed to join him in a pirate voyage — a very small crew for such a venture, but they expected to recruit others from captured vessels.

They conspired to seize a fine ship then lying in harbour at St. Pierre — a trading schooner belonging to William Minot of Boston. Apparently something went wrong with the plan, for on the night of August 29 only five of the conspirators actually showed up. Nevertheless, with courage worthy of a nobler cause, they decided to continue with their plan.

Luring the watchman from the deck, they bound and gagged him and left him on shore while they quietly slipped the cable, hoisted sail, and by dawn were hull down on the horizon. Once out of sight of land they held a meeting and signed a set of pirate articles.

The actual document that these five men signed on their first morning at sea is preserved in the Massachusetts archives — one of the few such documents in existence. It seems to prove that Phillips was a fairly literate man, although the fetish on which they took the oath, the blade of an axe since they lacked a Bible, does not argue a strong case for their religious training.

The articles they signed provided that deserters would be marooned — stranded on an uninhabited island — that thieves who stole from the company's communal loot would be marooned or shot, that anyone who endangered the ship or started a fight with a shipmate would be flogged, and that there would be compensation from the common store for those who lost limbs in battle. Rape or molestation of a woman was to be punished by death.

In some respects the pirates were ahead of their age. There was no compensation for injury in any other employment at the time.

The commonest punishment in Phillips's articles was "Moses's law on the bare back" — thirty-nine lashes prescribed for such crimes as carrying an uncovered candle or smoking an uncovered pipe below decks. It may seem to us hardly credible that men would vote such punishment for themselves, but it was hardly severe by the standards of the time, and when the pirates gave a shipmate a whipping they probably used something a good deal less deadly than the notorious cat-o'-nine-tails favoured by English naval captains and the magistrates on shore.

The names affixed to the pirate articles were John Phillips, John Nutt, Thomas Fern, James Sparkes, and William White. They renamed the ship the *Revenge* and proceeded to raid the fishing fleets on the Banks. In the following eight months they ran down and captured at least thirty-three ships, some of them armed and one that was actually fitted out for war, mounting twelve guns.

The original five were quickly joined by a full crew from captured ships — most of them volunteers, but some impressed to fill jobs that the volunteers were not qualified for. One of the new recruits turned out to be an already famous pirate named John Rose Archer, former lieutenant of the notorious Blackbeard who had been killed five years earlier in a frightful hand-to-hand conflict on the deck of a British sloop-of-war. Another early recruit was John Fillmore who not only escaped the gallows, but after his trial for piracy in Boston, founded an important family. John Fillmore's great-grandson, Millard Fillmore, became thirteenth President of the United States.

From an English ship captured a few days later the pirates received another enthusiastic recruit, a man named William Taylor, an English tradesman who had fallen into debt and was being sold into bondage on a Virginia plantation. Like Fillmore, he later became founder of an important family. Among the ships they took in the early days was the brigantine *Mary* under Captain Moore inward bound to Carbonear with a cargo valued at £500. They also took a French ship carrying more than a thousand gallons of wine.

With a full crew and plenty of provisions, they next sailed for the West Indies. But among the islands they had much worse luck than on the Banks. Piracy had almost stopped the West Indian trade at this point, and pickings had become lean. Their supplies were running low when they captured a French sloop-of-war and sailed it into Tobago for a refit. The cove where they careened their ship was a small, sheltered bay with a sand beach, plenty of fresh water, and dense jungle coming down to the sea on either side. At Tobago they captured another small vessel and began to fit her out for piracy.

There was now trouble in the ranks. Thomas Fern, one of the original company of five, conspired with four of the crew to take the small ship and head for the high seas on their own account. They almost got away, but Phillips pursued and captured them, brought them back, and held a trial. The four lesser pirates were pardoned and allowed to rejoin the crew, but they condemned Thomas Fern to death, tied him to a palm tree, and shot him through the heart, as the articles he had signed prescribed.

Fern had been ship's carpenter. To replace him Phillips chose Edward Cheeseman, the carpenter from a captured ship, the *Dolphin*, which they had taken on the Banks of Newfoundland. Cheeseman (impressed into the crew) had been conspiring from the start for Phillips's overthrow. Within a few weeks Cheeseman had a powerful confederate, a New England fishing skipper named Andrew Haradan.

It was April 1724 when Phillips seized Haradan's ship on the Banks. She was so new that parts of her topsides were actually unfinished, and men were still working on her decks with carpenter's tools while she pursued her fishing voyage. Since she was a better vessel than the one they were then using, the pirates transferred all their stores and loot to the captured ship and allowed the fishing crew to sail away empty-handed in the *Revenge*. But, perhaps because of his experience in seamanship and navigation, Haradan was forced to remain on board. It took him and Cheeseman less than three days to bring their plot for a mutiny to violent fruition.

First they moved all the carpenter's tools up on deck — a thing they could do without arousing suspicion because the decks were still not quite completed. Broadaxes, adzes, mallets, and hammers were left lying about where the conspirators could reach them in a hurry. Then they pretended to be busy under Cheeseman's direction while awaiting the signal from Haradan to attack the pirates at the most auspicious moment.

It came at noon on April 17, 1724. Phillips was below in his cabin. The conspirators seized John Nutt, the first mate, and flung him over the side. A moment later James Sparkes, the chief gunner and another of the original band of five, was stunned by a blow and dumped overboard. Hearing the commotion, Phillips rushed on deck. Cheeseman was waiting for him at the companionway with a large shipwright's caulking hammer. With this he delivered a blow to the head that broke Phillips's jaw. Nevertheless, the pirate grabbed a weapon and lunged for Cheeseman, but at that moment Haradan came up behind him and clove his skull with an axe. What was left of Phillips's head was then cut off as a trophy, and his body thrown overboard. Cheeseman next went below, laid out John Rose Archer with his trusty hammer, and herded the other pirates on deck. There the conspirators butchered ten of them and flung their bodies overboard, the remainder being bound and locked up to face trial ashore.

Andrew Haradan now resumed command of his own vessel and sailed her back to Massachusetts Bay in triumph, with Phillips's head hanging from a yardarm. He tied up at his home dock, sent seven chained pirates ashore to face trial, and had Phillips's head cured in a barrel of pickles, which he forwarded to Boston.

Cheeseman and Fillmore were tried for piracy and promptly acquitted. Fillmore, who had been in Newfoundland when the *Revenge* was first captured, then testified against the only survivor of the original five, William White. John Rose Archer, who had started life as a Newfoundland fisherman, served with Blackbeard, and finally as second officer under Phillips, was convicted on his record. He had been on the public "wanted" list for years.

Thirteen of the pirates had been killed on board ship. Most of the survivors were either acquitted or reprieved. Even William Taylor, who had turned pirate voluntarily to escape the life of a plantation slave, was first convicted and then pardoned. He subsequently settled in Newfoundland, where his family became honest planters and seamen.

John Rose Archer and William White were publicly hanged with all due ceremony, including a long oration from the Reverend Cotton Mather, the famous hanging parson of Boston whose greatest delight was to officiate at executions, whether of pirates or witches. The body of White was buried in the ordinary way, but Archer was hanged in chains on a small island in Boston Bay with the black flag of the *Revenge* bearing its white skeleton fluttering above him. Phillips's pickled head, hanging from a pole, was also exhibited on the Boston waterfront as a warning to visiting sailors.

CHAPTER 6
BARTHOLOMEW
ROBERTS

I T WAS EARLY June in the year 1720, and the little village of Trepassey on Newfoundland's south coast lay quiet in the light mist of predawn. Houses and stages and fishing stores crowded the shoreline. Here and there a merchant's premises stood out somewhat larger and better built than the small wooden houses of the fishermen. More than twelve hundred men and a few women lay in exhausted sleep, having worked from dawn the day before until midnight or even later splitting and cleaning and packing fish into salt, working under the reddish light of cod-oil lamps after daylight had failed.

It was the time of the "caplin scull" when billions of small silver fish, a species of sea smelt, crowded toward shore to spawn on the beaches, and the great schools of codfish crowded after them, feeding voraciously. Most of the season's catch of cod would be taken in the next few weeks in nets and on baited lines, and everyone worked to exhaustion, sometimes twenty hours at a stretch, to start the lengthy process of "shore cure" by which the fish were converted to the best grade of salted fillets that commanded the highest price in all the major ports of Europe.

There were just a few "planter" families at Trepassey, all of them recent arrivals, for the port had passed into English hands only seven years earlier when the French had finally given up their settlements in southern Newfoundland under the Treaty of Utrecht that ended the War of the Spanish Succession. The fishing crews were composed mainly of transients, men from western England and Ireland, but included a few women as cooks (but they worked at the fish, too, when they weren't cooking), and many young apprentices to the fish-curing trade.

In the harbour about 150 fishing smacks and shallops lay at anchor. In another hour they would be crowded with men and boys hurrying off to the fishing grounds just beyond the headlands. There were also twenty-two ships at anchor, mostly fishing and merchant vessels from Bristol, their crews on shore with the other fishermen, only their watchmen left in charge.

It was around 4:00 a.m., and the first light was staining the sky above the hills toward Biscay Bay when the peace of the sleeping village was shattered by a hellish uproar of gunfire and trumpets, a continuous cannonade accompanied by the blaring of brass horns. Up the long, narrow reach from the south, fire belching from every port, came a ship under full sail, a huge black flag with a white skeleton drinking a toast to death fluttering from her masthead.

The flag identified the pirate at once. This was none other than "Black Bart," the pirate who had spread fire and death along the coasts of Africa and North and South America, the most feared man of his time. His ship, the *Royal Rover*, had never been defeated in a sea fight. His most recent exploit was still the talk of the North Atlantic ports.

A few months earlier, while he was still supposed to be plundering the slave ships along the coast of the Gulf of Guinea in Africa, he had appeared off the coast of Brazil where a fleet of forty-two Portuguese merchant ships were at anchor guarded by two warships, preparing to sail for home. The *Royal Rover* had sailed straight into the middle of this fleet, selected the most prosperous-looking prizes, raked them with gunfire, boarded them, and carried off loot rumoured to be worth some ten thousand pounds. The helpless merchantmen had signalled frantically for the protection of the two warships, but by the time they had their anchors hoisted and their sails aloft, the *Royal Rover* was off and away before a fresh breeze, her trumpeters and fiddlers playing a merry tune, and her crewmen dancing on the decks.

News of this incredibly brazen raid had reached Newfoundland with the fishing schooners from New England more than a month before, but no one suspected that the *Royal Rover* was heading for Newfoundland. She had appeared off Canso a few days before and picked over the fishing fleet at her leisure, but no ship from Nova Scotia had since put in at Trepassey. The wealthy Bristol merchants who traded there, the stolid masters of fishing rooms, seamen, women, young boys on their first voyage away from home, all huddled on the foreshore like a flock of frightened fowl while the pirate ship bore down on the largest of the anchored merchant vessels, and the watchmen from the ships' decks fled in rowboats for the safety of the shore.

"Black Bart," perhaps the most flamboyant pirate who ever lived, was formerly the respectable Bartholomew Roberts, one of the most brilliant navigators of his time. Of Welsh parentage and working-class background, he had risen from a common sailor to first mate (sailing master) of a sloop trading to the West Indies. But no matter how great his ability, he would never make captain of a ship unless he was also its owner. Captains, in those days, did not rise from the ranks. He was a mere third mate of the *Princess*, taking slaves on the coast of Africa in June 1719, when she was captured by pirates and he was impressed into the crew.

The leader of the gang that captured Roberts was a famous Welsh pirate named Howell Davis. Six weeks after the capture Davis was dead, slain in an ambush by Portuguese slave traders, still on the coast of Guinea. The pirates escaped in their ship and in a conference at sea decided to offer Roberts the leadership. He proved his worth at once by leading them back to the Portuguese slaving station where Davis had been killed. In a furious surprise assault he sacked the small settlement and put it to the torch. Then off they went, capturing prizes along the coast of Africa. Tiring of this after a few weeks, they headed for the coast of Brazil and the great *coup* that made Roberts and the *Royal Rover* famous on both sides of the Atlantic.

Roberts kept an entire orchestra on his ship — trumpeters, drummers, and fiddlers who were required to play when going into battle and also to amuse the crew on any day except Sunday. As he headed for the centre of the fleet at Trepassey, the orchestra blared out a din of military music while the ship's thirty-two cannons and twenty-seven swivel guns roared away. Because they were meeting no resistance, the pirates didn't waste shot. They just stuffed the guns with as much powder as they would safely hold and set them off in a continuous cannonade designed to intimidate everyone within earshot.

There were no shore batteries at Trepassey to dispute the *Royal Rover*'s command of the harbour. If anyone dared to put off from shore in a boat, it could be sunk with ease. Roberts looted the anchored ships at his leisure. He sank a few fishing smacks and set fire to some of the ships, perhaps as a means of spreading more terror among the watchers or perhaps just from the love of arson.

As the day wore on, fishing and trading vessels began arriving from the Banks. One by one they sailed up the long, narrow bay leading into Trepassey Harbour. One by one Roberts bore down on them and took them prisoner, four ships in all, making a total of twenty-six that he captured in Trepassey. The crews he disarmed and sent ashore. The ships he looted of whatever valuables they contained.

One of the ships at anchor was a fine Bristol galley, probably well known to Roberts since she came from his home port. He decided to make her his flagship. He transferred to her the best of his armament and the most valuable bales of his loot and renamed her the *Royal Fortune*. Before he departed, he had three well-armed ships, for among the other loot he had captured from the anchored merchantmen were forty cannons and numerous swivel guns, with powder and shot for them.

The new flagship was a square-rigged three-master, flying about 3,000 square yards of canvas, and perhaps capable of a speed of fourteen knots under full sail with a strong wind. She was also provided with oars and oar ports so that she could be rowed if becalmed or if she found herself in narrow waters where sailing was impossible.

Before leaving Trepassey, Roberts decided to loot the shore stations of whatever useful goods they might possess. He began a bombardment of the merchants' premises, and sure enough, everyone fled to the woods and hills. The pirates landed almost unopposed. A few shots were fired at them from the shelter of nearby trees, and a few of the pirates may have been hit by musket balls. After looting the merchants' stores of everything they considered of value, they set fire to the stages and stores and rowed back to their ships, leaving Trepassey in flames.

The *Royal Fortune* then sailed off into Trepassey Bay, rounded Mistaken Point and Cape Race, and headed north along the shore past Renews, Ferryland, and Cape Broyle. The pirates on board were having a high old time with the puncheons of rum they had captured at Trepassey, but they found time to intercept and loot the cabins of all the fishing ships they met between Cape Race and Cape Spear.

A ship's most valuable cargo, including whatever money she carried, was usually stored in her "great cabin." Thus she could be fleeced rather easily. A brief inspection of the hold soon revealed whether she carried valuable cargo. If there was nothing but fish or salt, Roberts would depart with the captain's chest, leaving the ship and crew free to pursue their lawful occupations.

Here and there he took a recruit. Only rarely did he "enforce" anybody, and then only if the man was a tradesman whose talents he might need. From the *Blessing* of Lymington he received one of his most interesting volunteers, a twenty-two-year-old able seaman named John Walden.

This young pirate had many remarkable qualities. He was fearless, an excellent fighter, an expert seaman, and a good-looking man who soon became Robert's mate and bedfellow. The crew called him "Miss Nanny" behind his back, "Nanny" being eighteenth-century slang for a passive homosexual.

The term "mate" did not mean, as it would today, that Walden was second in command. It only meant that he was the captain's confidant and transmitted his orders. Other men, elected by the crew or appointed by Roberts, held more responsible positions such as sailing master, quarter-master (in charge of the common store of loot), and boat-swain (in charge of the deck).

The pirates usually elected all their officers and might change them at will, but Roberts, once in charge, was much more an authority figure than most pirate captains. Not only was he a renowned navigator, but he issued a standing invitation to any crewman who disagreed with him to go ashore and settle the issue in a duel. No one ever took him up on this, even though he once shot a defiant crewman dead on the deck.

He also dressed and acted like a gentleman, a man who expected to be obeyed. Instead of carousing on deck around the rum barrel with his fellow pirates, he sat alone in his cabin drinking tea. When going into action or receiving the surrender of a ship, he stood on his quarterdeck dressed in all the finery of a courtier: scarlet damask waistcoat and breeches, a hat with white plumes, pistols hung from silk sashes, and a diamond-studded gold cross with a gold chain. Even in battle he paced his deck in this conspicuous uniform, as though defying fate to strike him dead.

Some of his enemies called him a puritan — which he clearly was not — but he did seem to believe in the sobering effect of religion on the rough and superstitious gang over which he held sway. All hands were called together nightly to say prayers. The Sabbath was strictly observed as a day of rest. Even for swearing, a man was liable to be whipped.

These and other rules, their articles of war, were drawn up and agreed to democratically. Every man had an equal vote.

Among their articles were these:

No fighting on board ship. Quarrels to be settled ashore by duelling with pistols or cutlasses.

All to have equal shares, but clothing in addition if a man needed it.

Any who should defraud the company even of a single dollar should be marooned.

Any who should rob a shipmate should have his nose and ears split and be put ashore where he would be sure to suffer hardship.

No lights or candles after eight at night. Drinking at night only on deck and without lights.

No smoking of uncovered pipes or carrying of lighted candles below deck.

No gaming for money, either with dice or cards.

No boy or woman to be allowed among the crew. Any man seducing a woman and carrying her to sea in disguise should suffer death.

Most of these articles had nothing to do with morals, but were designed for the safety of the ship. Boys and women were not excluded because Roberts or anyone else on board objected to buggery and fornication — they revelled in such activities when they were ashore — but because they could easily become centres of jealousy and fighting.

Despite crimes that should have condemned him to the lowest level of hell, Roberts may well have considered himself religious. The cross he wore was probably a religious talisman. One of the ships he captured had a Protestant parson on board. He made every effort to persuade the clergyman to become chaplain to his crew. When the man steadfastly refused, Roberts had him released.

After scouting the Newfoundland coast and replenishing munitions, provisions, and crewmen, Roberts headed back to Nova Scotia. At that time Cape Breton Island and Quebec were still French. Cape Breton was the principal rendezvous of the French overseas fishing fleet, and here Roberts captured six large French vessels. One of them was an even finer ship than the recently acquired *Royal Fortune*, and she became the second ship of that name. Once again, the best cannons were transferred, together with Roberts's favourite furnishings. He now had crews sufficient for three ships (perhaps as many as four hundred men) and more loot than a single ship could carry, so Roberts fitted out two others — the *Great Ranger* and the *Little Ranger*. If a single sail of moderate size came into view, the *Great Ranger* would be ordered off alone to capture it, while the *Royal Fortune*, accompanied by the *Little Ranger*, was reserved for major exploits.

A few of the Frenchmen captured on the coast of Cape Breton Island were impressed into Roberts's crew since they were lucky enough to possess skills that he needed. They were not made sharemen with the pirates but were treated as slaves. The other captured Frenchmen were mostly slaughtered with vengeful ferocity. The Governor of Bermuda, reporting to Great Britain, said that some Frenchmen "were whipped nigh unto death," others had their ears docked, still others were hung by the hands from a yardarm and used for target practice. English prisoners, on the other hand, were usually released unharmed except for being stripped of anything that the pirates wanted. The most dreadful incident of Roberts's career occurred when they captured a ship containing eighty black slaves. The white crewmen escaped but the pirates burned the ship and roasted the slaves alive, still in their chains below decks.

Roberts could also be personally vengeful. Before arriving in Canada he had operated for a while in the Caribbean. There the Governor of Martinique (the most important of the French islands) made strenuous efforts to get naval ships to pursue him, and Roberts announced that sooner or later he would hang this man from a yardarm. He now headed south to the West Indies, paid a surprise visit to Fort-de-France, the capital of Martinique, sent a raiding party on shore, kidnapped the governor, and sailed away with his body dangling from his maintop yard.

The *Royal Fortune* lingered among the West Indian Islands as long as there was any loot to collect. Shipping came to a halt. No one dared send a valuable cargo to sea so long as the pirate squadron ranged the waters. They sailed where they willed, exchanged stolen goods for money and services, and spent their time in wild orgies with booze and women in Caribbean ports where pirates were regularly entertained by the local rabble of blackmarket merchants and whores. Most of their loot they took with them to be exchanged for gold in West Africa, which was to be their last landfall.

Early in the summer of 1721 the pirate fleet arrived on the coast of Senegal, the westernmost tip of Africa. Then they sailed southward to Sierra Leone, where they exchanged most of their captured goods for gold and enjoyed the hospitality of the English blackmarket merchants and free-lance slave traders who flourished there in a competition with the Royal Africa Company, which was supposed to enjoy a monopoly of English trade in West Africa.

Refreshed and refitted, the fleet then headed southward and eastward along the Guinea coast, where they captured a whole fleet of slave ships belonging to the Royal Africa Company and held them for ransom. The company paid up, but the two warships that they had secured from Britain to police the Guinea coast were soon on Roberts's trail.

The *Royal Fortune* by now mounted forty cannons, like a regular battleship, and Roberts was so used to defying governments and winning every skirmish that he shrugged off the presence of the two powerful British cruisers and remained on the Slave Coast collecting loot and carousing ashore long after he knew about them and could easily have escaped. By this time he had captured some four hundred merchant ships — the exact tally would never be accurately computed.

The warship that caught him was the *Swallow* under Captain Chaloner Ogle. He sighted Roberts's flotilla at anchor on the coast of Ghana and cleverly turned away, as though wishing to avoid them. Roberts, thinking the *Swallow* a merchant ship and an easy prize, sent the *Great Ranger* off in pursuit. Ogle drew the pirate far offshore, out of sight and sound of the other ships, then turned on her and battered her into submission without a single casualty among his crew. He sent her off to Cape Coast Castle, the headquarters of the Royal Africa Company, with a prize crew on board and the pirates in leg irons. Then he headed back to the place where he had sighted the *Royal Fortune*.

Five days after luring the *Great Ranger* out of her sight, Ogle caught up with the pirate flagship for the second time. He happened to meet her at the most opportune moment when her crew were helplessly drunk and hungover following an all-night debauch. Roberts, a teetotaller, was eating breakfast, and most of his crew were comatose on deck when he realized a warship was bearing down on him.

He changed into his scarlet, gold, and plumes, then rushed about the deck rousing as many pirates as possible to a state of semi-consciousness. Those who failed to respond he beat into wakefulness with the flat of his sword. By this means he managed to get the sails hoisted and the ship under steerage. Then, in an act of pure madness, instead of fleeing for his life he headed straight for the warship to do battle.

The two ships passed within point-blank range of each other and exchanged broadsides. The ragged fire of the drunken pirates did little damage to the *Swallow*, but the rigging and spars of the *Royal Fortune* were so torn and shattered that flight became impossible. The *Swallow* followed up this first exchange of fire by raking the decks of the *Royal Fortune* with grapeshot. Roberts was killed by the first rounds, and the crew utterly demoralized. Too late, they tried to flee. The *Swallow* came about hard on their heels, overtook them, and raked their decks with more grapeshot.

John Walden, Roberts's "mate," lost a leg in the battle,

but lived to be hanged. However, he managed to carry out Roberts's last wishes by throwing the captain's body, scarlet damask, white plumes, and all, over the side so it could not be hanged in chains from a gibbet on shore. Then the surviving pirates, many of them already dying, hauled down their flag and asked for quarter.

Besides those killed in action, the *Swallow* took 254 prisoners from the three ships and landed them at Cape Coast Castle in Ghana for trial and execution. They were housed in the "slave hole," a dungeon under one of the Royal Africa Company's forts, where nineteen of them died of wounds before the trial began.

Seventy-four prisoners, believed to be conscripts, were acquitted. Fifty-four others were sentenced to death, but two of those were later reprieved. Fifty-two were actually hanged, in batches, over a period of several days.

Twenty pirates were sentenced to a far worse death than hanging. They were sent into the Royal Africa Company's gold mines, where every one of them died under the overseers' whips. Seventeen were sentenced to prison and were shackled like slaves in the hold of a ship bound for England. Only four of them survived the voyage.

Captain Ogle stole the hoard of gold dust that he found in the cabin of the *Royal Fortune*. The rest of her cargo he turned over to the authorities. He returned to England both wealthy and famous and was given a knighthood for ending Roberts's rampage — the only English officer who was ever knighted for suppressing piracy. He eventually rose in the ranks to become an admiral.

CHAPTER 7
SEA WOLVES OF THE GOLDEN AGE

IN THE SEVENTEENTH and eighteenth centuries —
and even to a lesser extent in the nineteenth century
— war was the great prelude to piracy. Since no nation
maintained a truly powerful navy, governments had a habit,
the moment war broke out, of licensing privateers to prey on
enemy commerce, allowing them to keep most of the loot
they could capture. So profitable was this frightful trade
that corporations were organized for no other purpose than
fitting out fleets of privateers, and many private warships
were built specifically to go commerce-hunting among the
shipping lanes.

With the coming of peace, these private navies had no legal
employment. So, between wars, the seas swarmed with pirates.

From 1704 to 1713 approximately one hundred privateers flying the Cross of St. George and licensed by Good Queen Anne of Great Britain captured some two thousand French and Spanish ships, to the great profit of their captains and their owners. When this easy flow of wealth was cut off by the Treaty of Utrecht, the Golden Age of piracy followed.

One of the most colourful characters of this Golden Age was Captain Charles Bellamy. He has been called "the socialist pirate." But the name does not stand up to scrutiny. There seem to have been two Captain Bellamys sharing the Atlantic between them in 1717 or thereabouts. Neither of them was a socialist, but Samuel Bellamy may be said to have had some socialist leanings. He was not much of a pirate — his career lasted only a few months before he ran himself aground and drowned almost everyone on board his ship.

Charles Bellamy is first reported on the coast of New England and then in the Bay of Fundy in the early summer of 1717. His three ships scouted the north shore of the bay, what is now the coast of New Brunswick but was then regarded as part of the colony of Nova Scotia. Here they chose a safe, easily defended cove and made it their headquarters.

The location is uncertain, but such description as we have suggests St. Andrew's, a harbour well protected by reefs and islands with a river flowing into it, good pine timber for building and for the repair of ships, and well off the shipping routes between the New England and the Newfoundland colonies. Here the pirates built not only a careenage on which to clean and repair their ships but also a fort with a breastwork and gun emplacements. Well separated from the rest, a powder magazine was constructed, where their stores of shot and their barrels of black powder would be safe from accident or attack.

Bellamy was a good organizer and was able to undertake this ambitious project because he had plenty of slave labour at his command. He had captured the crews of several ships farther south, and the pirates stripped the prisoners naked and drove them with whips "after the same manner as the Negroes are used by the West Indian Planters" (Defoe).

While the chain gangs toiled in the sun, Bellamy and his lieutenants lay about sipping rum and discussing plans for founding a new nation with Bellamy as its president and his associate pirates as chief ministers. This romantic nonsense must have seemed vaguely possible at the time and place, hundreds of miles from any of the established colonies but in the same region where the French had successfully founded Acadia more than a hundred years before.

With everything shipshape once more, Bellamy's fleet next crossed the great bay to Yarmouth, then headed out around Cape Sable and northward and eastward over the western fishing banks to a temporary anchorage in Fortune Bay on Newfoundland's south coast. Here they captured and sank a number of fishing and trading ships and enlisted some of the crews as pirates. Then they scattered, looking for prey.

Bellamy's ship headed into the Gulf of St. Lawrence where he sighted the sail of a large vessel heading westward and gave chase. He came up with the ship in late afternoon, French by her colours, probably carrying both money and supplies for the trading posts at Tadoussac or Quebec.

The ship came about, hoisted her ports, and ran out a formidable array of cannons. She was, in fact, a warship

mounting thirty-six guns, carrying soldiers to the fortress
at Quebec. Bellamy immediately realized that he was in
mortal danger and tried to escape, but the French ship was
a good sailor and could run both on and off the wind fully
as well as the pirate. Grapeshot and canister shot ripped
through Bellamy's rigging. Heavy balls came tearing across
the deck, carrying everything before them. He replied with
his own guns in a battle that lasted for three or four hours.
Fortunately for Bellamy, darkness was falling and a rain-
storm was coming on. He escaped being captured or sunk,
but his ship was badly mauled, and thirty-six of his men
were killed.

He limped back to Newfoundland waters, found sanctuary on the west side of Placentia Bay, and set up a new
careenage where his fleet reassembled and the ships were
repaired. Again, the exact location of this pirate fort is
unknown. It was certainly not at Placentia, as some writers have said (confusing the former French fortress, by that
time in the hands of an English garrison, with the bay of the
same name), but may well have been at Oderin, a beautiful haven among islands on the opposite shore where the
sunken remains of ancient marine works can still be seen —
slipways and the like — that cannot be accounted for by any
marine works known to history.

According to the pirate historian Philip Gosse, Charles
Bellamy continued to prowl the western Atlantic for nine
years and assembled a fleet in Newfoundland as late as
1726. This, however, may be an error, for Gosse, like
Daniel Defoe before him, attributes the short-lived career
of Captain Samuel Bellamy to the apparently much more
successful Charles.

Unlike Charles who simply disappears (and probably retired, like many other pirates, with a comfortable nest egg), Samuel can be neatly fitted into the months between February 1716, when he was a legitimate salvage operator in the West Indies, and April 1717, when his ship foundered near Cape Cod and he and nearly all his crewmen were drowned. Because a few of them lived to be hanged, the crewmen who sailed with Samuel Bellamy left a detailed record in the court proceedings of Massachusetts, and because of these documents we can eliminate many of the stories that have gathered around Bellamy's name.

If the speeches published by Daniel Defoe were ever made at all, then they were made by Samuel Bellamy, not by Charles. These speeches, often reprinted, were undoubtedly written by Defoe, but there is some slight background for them in the evidence produced at the trials. "They rob the poor under cover of law. We plunder the rich under the protection of our own courage," thunders Defoe's Bellamy at the captain of a captured ship whom he is trying to convert to piracy. Nothing quite like this was quoted in court, but the Bellamy who emerges there from the tangled evidence is at least the kind of man who might have said something of the sort.

The story that he was intentionally led ashore by the captain of a captured whaler is not true either. His ship ran aground because of his own lack of navigational skill and was soon buried under many thousands of tons of sand. But not before she was stripped by local wreckers, some of whom were hailed before court in an unsuccessful attempt by the Government of Massachusetts to recover a share of the loot.

In 1982 an American salvage company, one of whose

members was the son of the late President John Kennedy, reported that they had located Samuel Bellamy's ship and were preparing to recover the vast treasure that they were sure it contained. Whether, in fact, the wreckers of 1717 left such a treasure in her cabins or holds or wherever it was supposed to be would seem, at best, to be doubtful.

In any case, Charles Bellamy never grounded on the Nantucket Shoals, never had any of his crewmen tried for piracy in Boston, and was not, so far as any contemporary records reveal, stranded on the coast of Massachusetts in 1726 or at any other time.

During Bellamy's reputedly long career there were a number of minor pirate captains, some of them associated with him, also operating in the waters of Eastern Canada.

George Lowther was captain of one such ship and took a number of fishing and trading vessels as prizes, most of them along the coast of Newfoundland. In 1723 he sailed to the West Indies and put his ship on careenage there. With her guns dismounted and the ship hove down for cleaning, Lowther had the bad luck to be caught by the South Sea Company's armed merchant vessel *Eagle*.

Most of the pirates were taken prisoner and condemned to lifelong slavery, some in the galleys, others on the West Indian plantations. Lowther himself escaped with three other men and a small boy, but a few days later he was found dead with his pistol beside him. The handgun was said to have misfired and exploded. So perhaps he died accidentally. Others said he deliberately shot himself. But there was never any investigation of his death. He may well have been killed by one of the other escaped pirates.

Another notorious ruffian of the period was Thomas Anstis

who captured the ship on which John Phillips was a passenger in 1721 as she headed in over the Banks of Newfoundland.

Anstis (the archetypal fiend who tortured, raped, and murdered his prisoners) was master of the *Good Fortune*, a name borne by many pirate vessels. When he captured the larger and faster *Morning Star*, a ship out of Bristol in the Newfoundland trade, he gave command of the *Good Fortune* to his mate, Brigstock Weaver, and headed south for the West Indies in the larger ship.

The two ships met again at Tobago where Anstis put the *Morning Star* on careenage and, like Lowther, was caught by a warship. Forty of the pirates were captured, but Weaver and Phillips were among those who escaped into the woods, barefooted and empty-handed, while all their loot and personal possessions were confiscated. The marines from the warship found Anstis dead in his hammock, apparently murdered by one of his own crew.

Phillips later got work on a merchant ship, and Weaver also managed to return to England where he was seen two years later, a barefoot beggar seeking alms in Bristol. He was recognized by a merchant captain whose ship had been seized by Anstis and denounced to the authorities. Arrested and taken to London, he was tried, convicted, and hanged at Execution Dock.

The longest career of any pirate of the Golden Age was that of Captain Lewis (first name unrecorded). Although many pirates of the seventeenth and eighteenth centuries carried young boys in their ships, Lewis was the first such waif to achieve notoriety and the distinction of becoming a pirate leader.

Lewis was only about ten years of age when he was on

Captain Bannister's ship, which was raiding merchant ships off Jamaica in 1687. When the vessel was run down and captured by an English warship commanded by Captain Spragge, Bannister and the other pirates were hanged from the yardarm, presumably after a brief courtmartial. But Spragge, rather surprisingly at a time when children were often hanged for very minor crimes, took pity on Lewis and another young boy, and instead of hanging them by the neck like their older shipmates, he hanged them by their middles from his mizzen topmast, took them into Port Royal, and released them, thoroughly terrified but physically unharmed.

Apparently well-chastened by this treatment, Lewis worked on ships sailing out of Port Royal as a ship's boy and ordinary seaman "till he was a lusty lad." Then a ship on which he was sailing was captured by Spanish raiders and taken to Havana.

Lewis remained in Cuba as a Spanish slave for a number of years, but eventually he and six other captives managed to escape in a canoe to a wild part of the Cuban coast where they joined other escaped captives and set up as small-time outlaws, stealing from the Cuban plantations, raiding ships whenever they could, gradually building up a store of arms and ammunition until they were strong enough to attack and capture a sloop mounting twelve guns. With this ship they set themselves up as regular pirates, elected Lewis as their leader, and sailed northward.

By now Lewis was in his late thirties, a man of experience and talents. As a sailor out of Jamaica he had learned navigation and seamanship. His adventures had made him fluent in both English and Spanish, and somewhere he had learned to speak French and one or more of the dialects then current among West Indian natives.

He and his crew went pirating off the coast of Florida, which was at that time still Spanish, and then off the Carolinas, which had flourishing English colonies. At last they arrived in Newfoundland, where they put their heavily armed sloop on careenage for cleaning and repair and finally sailed boldly into Trinity in Bonavista Bay, a splendid harbour and a centre of the fishery where Sir Richard Whitbourne, a century earlier, had convened the first Vice-Admiralty Court outside the realm of England.

When Lewis sailed into Trinity the fishing fleet was at anchor and very lightly manned, most of the crews being at work on the fishing stations ashore. The pirates went through the fleet at leisure, taking whatever they wanted from the ships and replacing their twelve-gun sloop with the finest English ship in the fleet — the twenty-four-gun *Herman*.

But among those on the shore stations was a Bristol captain named Woodes Rogers, father of the Woodes Rogers who became governor of the Bahamas and the greatest scourge of pirates in his time. Rogers got his fellow captains together and laid a plan to trap Lewis and his crew.

Trinity is a closed harbour with a narrow run into the sea and a point of land from which the entrance can be covered by shore batteries. There was already a rudimentary fort on this point, probably neglected and certainly without guns, but some of the guns from the fleet had been dismounted and taken ashore. There was also a magazine with plenty of shot and powder. Rogers and the other captains managed to move the guns to the fort, mount them, and cover the entrance. Since Lewis felt quite secure and was in no hurry, they probably had three or four days in which to accomplish their task. They now thought they had the pirates trapped.

The manoeuvre would likely have succeeded had Lewis not been favoured with a dark and moonless night. Quietly his crew hoisted sail and made a run for it. The ships' crews at the fort were expecting just this and had their guns primed and ready. They fired round after round at the pirate ship as she slipped quickly past on the ebb tide. They could hear the shot strike. But the *Herman* kept on, and vanished into the darkness, although somewhat disabled with "many shot into her hull," according to the report they sent to St. John's.

With daylight they sent off a fast packet to St. John's, where Captain Tudor Trevor was at anchor in the British warship *Sheerness*. It took the packet two days to make port, and the warship a few more hours to make sail and clear the harbour. Meanwhile, lookouts on Signal Hill reported that the pirate ship had sailed past, well out to sea, heading southward. The warship set off in pursuit, some four hours after the *Herman* was out of sight, but meanwhile the *Herman* had vanished into one of the numerous hidden coves along the coast.

There is one such mooring place about five or six hours' sail south of St. John's at a harbour named Cape Broyle — a safe mooring completely invisible from the sea where rings were formerly fastened into the solid stone cliffs, and a ship could lie in deep water moored fore and aft as though in dry dock.

When the warship had called off the chase, Lewis slipped out to sea once more, rounded Cape Race, and sailed along the south coast of Newfoundland. He hovered off the coast for two weeks until he was able to surprise and capture in harbour a large French ship that had been used as a privateer in the recent War of the Spanish Succession.

This ship, like the *Herman*, mounted twenty-four guns, but was a faster sailer and capable of mounting even more armament. Lewis transferred his best armament to her, enlisted some of her crew, and set off for the coast of Africa, where some of the best pirate pickings were to be found, provided you had a strong, well-armed ship.

He made the ocean passage without incident and prowled along the coast of Guinea, where he "captured a great many ships, English, Dutch and Portuguese."

By now Lewis was chief of an unwieldy organization, a robber band consisting of English and French crews working three or four ships at a time. They soon split into factions and began to quarrel. After a while, the English and the French crewmen divided, took separate ships, and agreed to go their separate ways. But they were unable to resist raiding each other. In one such raid Lewis was killed by the French faction, and his crews eventually disappeared.

Despite research by several historians of piracy, not much is known about Lewis's early life. He was probably of English descent, although this is by no means certain, and he was between thirty-eight and forty years old at the time of his death. Beyond that, nothing is known except for a few incidents from his childhood, his captivity and escape from Cuba, and the massive pirate raid that he carried out in Newfoundland.

Of all the many pirates who swarmed over Canadian seas in the so-called Golden Age, none was more vicious than Eric Cobham, unless it was his wife and partner in piracy,

Maria Lindsey. It seems that they killed for sport, followed a policy of leaving no survivors to bear evidence, and, according to Cobham's own account, managed to get away with piracies spread over a period of twenty years.

The Cobhams' favourite base was in the Gulf of St. Lawrence, although they occasionally raided farther south. According to tradition, their fort and careenage was in Bay St. George, at a place called Sandy Point. There, early in the eighteenth century, they were safe from detection except by occasional French or Basque crews of fishermen and a few aboriginals and French colonists who had strayed northward from the colony of Acadia.

Eric Cobham was born in Poole, one of the Channel ports of England, and went to sea as a boy. He may well have been engaged in the Newfoundland fisheries at the age of fourteen or fifteen, but by his late teens he was a member of a smuggling gang running brandy from France to England. One operation that he took part in was reported to have landed ten thousand gallons of spirits successfully.

At about the age of nineteen or twenty he was caught, flogged, and sent to Newgate Prison, where he spent some two years. On his release he got a job working at an inn in Oxford. There he succeeded in robbing one of the wealthy transients of a bag of gold coins. The innocent innkeeper was hanged for the theft, while Cobham moved south to Plymouth and bought a small ship.

Like many ships of her time, the vessel was armed. Cobham recruited a crew of desperadoes from the docks, probably many of them his former associates in the smuggling trade, and set off on a career of piracy.

Rounding The Lizard and heading northward to see

what pickings might be found in the Irish Sea, they ran into a great stroke of luck — an East Indiaman heading up the channel toward Bristol, carrying cargo worth forty thousand pounds, some of it in gold. Most pirates would have retired on the spot. Not Cobham. He scuttled the ship and drowned the crew, showing already the ruthlessness that marked his later career. Then he headed for the French Mediterranean ports to establish contacts with pirate brokers. There he sold his stolen goods and returned to Plymouth as a successful soldier of fortune.

In Plymouth he met Maria Lindsey and formed with her a partnership that lasted the rest of their lives. There is no record of their ever being churched, but they were certainly wedded. Shortly after they met, they enlisted a fresh crew of renegades and sailed for the New World.

They made landfall at Nantucket and captured their first transatlantic prize there. Then they cruised northward until they found their way past the tip of Cape Breton Island and discovered the supply route to Quebec where money going upriver and furs coming downriver provided a rich killing ground virtually untouched by other pirates.

The harbour that they chose for their careenage was far enough north of the shipping lanes to be safe from accidental discovery. The great walrus hunts that had reddened the waters of the Gulf of St. Lawrence a hundred and two hundred years before were now over. South of the Straits of Belle Isle the walrus was almost extinct, and except for the trade route that ran past the island of Cape Breton and the Perce Rock to Tadoussac and Quebec, the Gulf lay quiet. No one was likely to follow them into Sandy Point, or if he did, to find his way safely past the mass of shoals that guarded it from the sea. The long sand spit that curves around Flat Bay just south of St. George's great closed barachois would later become the "capital" of western Newfoundland, an important naval base, and a centre for the Gulf and Labrador fisheries, but all this was far in the future.

From St. George's Bay the pirates could reach their favourite theatre of operations around Cape Breton and Prince Edward Island (then called the Isle of St. John or Isle St. Jean) in two days' sail. They were within striking distance of all the traffic going to what are now the Maritime provinces of Canada and all the St. Lawrence traffic in and out of New France, most of which now moved through Cabot Strait, although some still moved by way of the Straits of Belle Isle.

At that time the Canadian fur trade was immensely valuable, and the price of the individual furs was rising. Certain varieties, then or a little later, were literally worth their weight in gold. The trade had been subject, from its inception more than two centuries before, to hijacking.

The Cobhams merely refined this art and added their own brand of ruthlessness. Everything that they captured, they sold in the Mediterranean ports, but rather than risking frequent Atlantic crossing themselves, they probably shipped their loot second-hand by way of traders who picked up cargoes at Perce. It was said that at Perce, in season, you could buy or sell anything from beaver pelts to crown jewels.

Cobham later boasted that he had operated for twenty years without ever being caught, but this probably included the later years of respectability up to his last coup in the English Channel. He attributed this good fortune to his policy of leaving no survivors. "Dead cats don't mew," the pirates used to say, but few pirates of the eighteenth century could bring themselves to operate with the Cobhams' thoroughness. Not until a hundred years later did piracy usually include massacre. The Cobhams murdered all hands and sank the ships, which were then listed as missing, without survivors, and presumed lost at sea.

The stories of Maria Lindsey's behaviour as a pirate strongly suggest homicidal insanity. She poisoned one ship's crew, had others sewn into sacks and thrown overboard alive, still others tied up and used for pistol practice. Such are the stories later told by her husband, uncorroborated by witnesses, but quite possibly true.

When the Cobhams judged that their wealth had grown sufficiently, they sailed for France, disposed of their final ships and cargoes, and bought a fine estate near Le Havre from the Duc de Chartres. They also bought a yacht in which they sailed on the Baie de la Seine and along the French shore of the English Channel.

They now had a private harbour, servants, and a respectable place among the landed gentry. But even then Cobham could not resist temptation when it fell his way. On one cruise he found a brig becalmed in the channel, inward bound from the West Indies to England, and apparently defenceless. Stealing on board, he and his servants took the crew by surprise, overpowered them, murdered them, and dumped them in the sea. He then sent both ship and cargo to Bordeaux to be sold.

Cobham, wealthy squire and landowner, pillar of respectability, was appointed magistrate, a judge in the French county courts, a position that he held for twelve years.

But he and Maria gradually became estranged. He took to almost public wenching. She took to alcohol often laced with laudanum. While he made a reputation for himself as a lover, she became more withdrawn and solitary.

Then, one day, she was missing. Her husband reported it and instigated a search, and after two days her body was found in the sea below a cliff. A doctor certified that she had taken enough laudanum to kill herself, and she was assumed to have leaped over the cliff as insurance against failure in suicide. This seems probable because Cobham, when he later confessed to everything else, did not include Maria's murder among his many crimes.

He died a natural death. When his end was near, he called a priest and made a lengthy confession, had the story of his life committed to writing, and asked that it be published.

His wishes were carried out, and the priest saw that the little book dictated by the ex-pirate was published, but Cobham's heirs, by now a respectable family, tried to suppress it, buying and burning every available copy. One somewhat defective copy found its way into the French archives, and this is the only primary source on Cobham. But he also had his biographer, who supplied other details, presumably from people who knew the pirate in his early or late career and possibly from some who served under him in the days when he hovered, a veritable angel of death, beside the supply line that ran between France and Canada.

CHAPTER 8
SAILING AGAINST NEW FRANCE

RIVATEERS WERE NOT INTENT on slaughter. Capturing ships and annoying the enemy were their *raison d'être*. But there were rare exceptions to this: life-and-death struggles with no thought except survival. And there were instances when equally matched ships tangled and fought it out. One such battle took place in April 1757, the year after the decisive struggle for North America had broken out between the English and the French. That year the armed merchant vessel *Robuste* was freighted for Quebec by the French government, armed with twenty-four guns and a crew of seventy-seven. She also carried 150 soldiers to reinforce the army of New France under General Louis-Joseph, Marquis de Montcalm.

On April 13, Captain Jean Joseph Rosier fell in with "an English frigate of thirty guns in a battery and a half." No privateer would engage a frigate by choice, but this was a case of mistaken identity, as Rosier's own account of the battle makes clear:

> *At daybreak I saw a vessel on my lee, heading northwards, the wind west-northwest, carrying four principal sails, her mizzen, and mizzen-topsail, without top-gallant masts. She changed her course to my wake, and approached. I put her down for a merchantman, obliged to approach by tacking. Her greater speed brought her, at noon, within a twelve-pound gunshot. Observing her closely I could then see that she was a frigate with a battery and a half of guns, crowded with men, and extraordinarily high in the water. Being unable to withdraw, and thinking it useless to parley, I clewed up by lower sails to await him. When he stood across my course I showed him my colours and, as is customary, fired a shot. He broke out his, accompanied by his full broadside. Then the fight began, and was most bloody, always side by side until 7 o'clock, when our mutual disarray forced us to draw off to set things to rights. I had my main [yard] and main-topsail smashed, my mizzen [yard] and foretopsail yard brought down, all my sails in rags, and useless. In this attack I had 18 killed instantly, and 42 wounded, several mortally, and several cannon shot just above the waterline.*
>   *Our plight seemed so bad that on making examination of the ship I agreed with my staff that we should turn back because of the impossibility*

of making repairs at sea. Consequently I set my course for Perthuis, or the River of Bordeaux, the wind being favourable, continuing all day and the next night under easy sail.

Around noon on the 15th my lookout saw a vessel about four leagues to leeward which was manoeuvring so as to approach me. My few sails did not permit me to avoid him; by 6 o'clock in the evening he was within range of a long-gun. He showed a white flag and fired a shot [but] not observing that he showed any special sign of need, I kept on my course. I took his bearing at sunset, and thought he was in my wake, and the flares and rockets which he was firing made me think he was in pursuit. At nine he was within earshot, and hailed me. I answered him. He said to me, in a compassionate tone: 'Poor prisoner, I advise you to surrender and not make any resistance. I will give you good terms.' His exhortation was followed by his broadside into my stern, which was exposed, his sails giving him an advantage over me. Consequently I manoeuvred my ship so that she was broadside to him. Then the battle became general, stem to stern, and was more savage, though less fatal, than the former one. In this attack, which ended at 1 o'clock in the morning, I had my main [topmast] and mizzen topmast smashed, my sails more destroyed than the earlier ones, 5 men killed and 11 wounded. My enemy, drawing off, allowed me to make repairs, which I did promptly. I refitted my mizzen and foretop-gallant yards, these being the only ones I could rig to keep me under way, which I did.

At daybreak my enemy, who had watched me all night, manoeuvred to rejoin me, which he managed by 11 o'clock. I recognized him as the same frigate with which I had had my first affray. I counted his guns, which were 15 on each side, and some of my officers assured me that they had seen cannon on his forecastle and quarter-decks. The engagement began anew, and did not cease until 6 o'clock, when he hailed, and I answered. He said to me, Yield, gentlemen, yield. You will be treated as you deserve. We will grant you good terms. We are an English King's frigate, so be contented.' Then he hoisted a square flag to his foretop. I answered, being unable to hoist a square flat like him, because I had no mast standing, that I was flattered to have conversation with my peers, that I still had powder and shot, that I much regretted I had no canvas to show him a course contrary to that which he would oblige me to take, and that if he would continue to do his duty, I would continue to do mine. I gave him three Vive le Roi, *my broadside of guns and musketry, at which we continued until half-past seven. My enemy, as crippled as I, was pumping water out of all his scuppers, and was steering with sweeps. I assumed his rudder was useless, and at the same time discovered that mine was also damaged. I had it repaired promptly. It was now out of the question for either to yield to the other. Our condition permitted us to think only of ourselves. The following night put us out of sight of each other.*

"I worked hard to manage the repairs. At daybreak I saw a ship ahead, approaching us. We came together at ten, and I made him out to be a privateer of 16 guns, and several swivels, with a large crew. He opened fire, but drew away after an hour, setting his lower sails before a following wind, discouraged by our response and

our gunnery. In those last two attacks we had 3 killed and 8 wounded. At noon I sighted the land near Oleron. At eight that evening I dropped anchor a league from Chassiron.

My state is much to be pitied. I have my mizzenmast standing, and that without its topmast, and my bowsprit, not a piece of rigging in working order from stem to stern, at least fifty shots near the waterline and a great number in the hull. I believe on both sides 3,000 shots were fired, and 15,000 rounds of musketry, which I verified by counting the cartridges remaining. I had 29 soldiers and seamen killed, and 61 wounded...

The captain then goes on to commend the ship's officers and officers of the regiment, who had shown great courage during the battle, some of them while wounded. Some of those wounded had been shot in the thigh. In those days, if the bone was shattered, this injury would require amputation, with only a 50 per cent chance of survival. A passenger, who was going to Quebec on government service, also died of wounds.

The captain explained that he had put up as gallant a fight as possible, "not being ignorant of the importance of my cargo to the King's service." Shipping into Quebec was indeed at a critical point that year. New France was very nearly starved into submission two years before the famous battle on the Plains of Abraham, and some three hundred people actually died of starvation in what was left to France of her former Acadian colony.

There is an interesting postscript to this skirmish in the battle for Canada. John Stewart McLennan, the Cape Breton historian who wrote a monumental history of Louisbourg, researched the British public records and the British press of 1757, looking for confirmation from those on the other side of the battle. What he found was that no frigate of the Royal Navy was in a position to have taken part in this battle and that there is no mention of it in British naval records, as there should have been. He did discover, however, a dispatch in the *London Chronicle*, dateline Bristol, May 7. It quoted a letter from an officer on board the Bristol privateer *Caesar*, describing an engagement with "a French frigate of thirty-six guns on the 13th, 15th and 16th of April . . . which was very obstinate and continued seven hours the last day; and when the *Caesar* left her she looked like a wreck, having lost all her masts and rigging." The *Caesar* reported only one man killed and twenty-two wounded (but this is a press account in wartime, not an official report, so we may take those statistics with a grain of salt.) More to the point, the letter reported that the *Caesar* had fired off seven hundred cannon shot and eight thousand musket rounds "besides an incredible number of Largin and Partridge shot." Also "three thirty Hand Grandes out of the tops, which did great execution." McLennan could not identify the "Hand Grandes." Perhaps they were fire pots, which the French captain reported were thrown to his deck from the topmasts of the English "frigate," though, according to his account, they did no serious damage, being caught and thrown into the sea by the promptness and bravery of his officers.

In any case, it turned out that this battle royal was between two privateers, with approximately equal gunning, each of which believed the other to be a naval frigate.

Privateers were absolutely crucial to the defence of New

France in the unequal fight with the British, in which the French colonists were outnumbered by at least ten to one, and the British always had superiority at sea. Morpain, captain of the Port of Louisbourg, commanded his own privateering vessel. Doloboratz was engaged as commander of another privateer to carry out the French attack on the British outpost at Canso. These two were the only ships of war sailing out of Louisbourg in 1744.

After successfully attacking Canso, Captain Doloboratz went on a privateering cruise along the coast of New England. He was well armed with twelve cannon and twelve swivels but quickly fell prey to a ship named the *Prince of Orange*, commissioned by the Colony of Massachusetts. There was much gunfire, but no one on either side was killed or injured in the battle. That same summer the Canso privateers captured nine vessels on the Banks of Newfoundland and one Irish merchant ship, but the English got much the better of the engagement. They sent out a raider named the *Kinsale*, armed with forty-four guns under Captain Robert Young. She arrived at St. John's, Newfoundland, June 23, having taken five ships en route, then raided the entire French shore between Cape Ray and Placentia, putting all the French fishing stations to the torch, including the fortified station of St. Pierre. She then turned her attention to the French fishery north of Cape Bonavista, where she sank or captured a number of French ships and took eighteen thousand quintals of fish, together with eighty tuns of oil.

During this war the New England colonies laid the foundations of the great tradition of privateering that served them so well against Louisbourg, and, a generation later, against the British in their War of Independence. The shipyards of Rhode Island, Massachusetts, and Pennsylvania worked at top speed building privateers and managed to get forty-nine of them at sea in the first year. One of them, sailing out of Boston, was reported at Louisbourg to have taken seventeen ships and seven hundred prisoners and to have sunk a thousand French fishing boats.

Most of the damage must have been to the French floater fishery in the Gulf of St. Lawrence. All the French fishing stations on the Gaspé, as well as in Newfoundland, went up in smoke and flame that year. The following summer the British colonies increased their privateering fleet to 113. They now outnumbered French privateers ten to one.

That was the year General William Pepperrell launched his attack on Louisbourg at the head of the colonial militia. His army of amateur soldiers would never have dared attack the great French fortress except for the support of a huge privateering fleet, commanded by Captain Edward Tyng, the first naval officer to be commissioned by the colony of Massachusetts and the man who had captured Doloboratz the year before. Pepperrell also had knowledge, gleaned in prisoner exchanges (again by way of privateering), that Louisbourg was badly defended, half-starving, and in danger of mutiny.

This amateur army of farmers and fishermen, supported by an amateur navy, sailed for Cape Breton without the support of any regular British troops, army officers, or any elements of the Royal Navy. The head of the British naval squadron in the West Indies gave it about as much chance of success as the Children's Crusade. But when new orders came from England to the West Indies squadron to proceed northward to "attack and distress the enemy in their settlements and annoy their fisheries and commerce," Commodore Peter Warren, British commander-in-chief for North America, set sail with three regular warships, two small armed vessels, and ten transports. A small force, indeed, to protect an expedition against the New World's strongest fortress. But when the British learned that the colony of Massachusetts, with some help from its neighbours, was actually attacking Louisbourg, they dispatched eight more warships to give support. The British squadron arrived off Louisbourg ahead of supply ships from France and imposed a blockade. When the supply fleet did arrive, only one small ship managed to slip through and shelter under the guns of the fort.

Louisbourg was starved into surrender after a siege of a month and a half. Pepperrell had accomplished the impossible by the promptness of his attack, even though his drunken "army" scarcely deserved the name and was certainly incapable of any serious fighting. When they entered Louisbourg, his undisciplined, ragtag militia broke out in an orgy of riot, pillage, and rape, and privateers and militiamen filled their chests with loot. From their point of view the adventure had been a great success, no matter what happened to the rocky island of Cape Breton. And of course, in the peace treaty the English handed Louisbourg back to the French, just as they had handed back Quebec in the previous century.

When the war against New France got going once more in 1756, no fewer than eighteen letters of marque were issued to privateers sailing out of Halifax, carrying among them 232 cannon and crews of 965 men. So attractive was privateering to the unskilled men of the town that Governor

Lawrence complained it was no longer possible to hire local labourers to keep the fortifications in repair. Labourers left town, lured by the promises of prize money held out by the recruiting officers of privateering companies, most of them partnerships entered into by shipowners to spread the risks of loss. New France also outfitted privateers, one of them, the *Caribou*, built at Quebec especially for the job. But in the western Atlantic the French were completely outgunned, both by private and commissioned warships. There was never anything like equality at sea.

In the end New France was defeated in battles fought on land, but it was a bloody, expensive business that need never have happened at all. It was only the arrival of a French supply fleet in the spring of 1759 that enabled Quebec to hold out as long as it did. Had the British wintered their ships at St. John's and Halifax, with orders to blockade Louisbourg and the St. Lawrence River as soon as navigation opened in the spring, there would have been no need for the brutal ravaging of the countryside by General James Wolfe's army or for the bloodletting on the Plains of Abraham. Had the British repeated the strategy of the privateer fleet under David Kirke, Canada would have fallen into their hands intact, and Wolfe would have missed his moment of glory.

CHAPTER 9
THE SPIRIT OF '76

I THE YEARS OF THE PIRATES" still fresh in the folk memory of Canada's Atlantic provinces are, strangely enough, years of glory celebrated in American history. The "pirates" in question were privateers carrying letters of marque from some embryo American state or other, occasionally even from the Continental Congress. But since some of them specialized not in attacking merchant ships but in raiding towns and villages and in campaigns of pillage through the countryside, they are remembered as pirates not only in folklore but in most of the documents of the time.

When the War of Independence erupted in 1775, the rebellious colonies expected Nova Scotia, and perhaps even Newfoundland, to join in their campaign to throw off the yoke of the King. When this failed to happen, they turned loose a swarm of raiders against the "Tories" of the north. Anyone not bearing arms against Great Britain was a legitimate target: his jewellery, money, and silverware free to be seized in a swift night attack, or his house burned at dawn.

The American naval historian D.W. Knox estimates that the American colonies issued letters of marque to some two thousand ships (all but a handful of them converted merchant ships) with eighteen thousand guns and seventy thousand men, not all serving at once but at sea throughout some part of the war. Some ships prowled along distant shores. Some fought out of French ports in the home waters of Great Britain. Others hugged the coastline of North America, raiding fishing settlements as far away as Labrador, carrying off cargoes of salt cod and barrels of oil, sinking small boats, and burning fish stages. Their most lucrative raids were in Nova Scotia, against the wealthy outports and the comfortable farms of the Annapolis Valley.

Though the rebels certainly got the better of the war at sea, they didn't have things entirely their own way. Michael Francklin, Joshua Mauger, and Malachi Salter were all privateering merchants operating out of Halifax in 1758, and Alexander Brymer owned a ship named the *Halifax* that he armed and equipped to raid rebel shipping. The *Revenge* and the *Liverpool* were two others that brought prizes to the Nova Scotia capital.

Then there was the *Lucy*, sailing out of Liverpool after the economy of that port had been all but ruined by rebel depredations. A committee of merchants got together, outfitted her, and raised a crew under Captain Freeman (a name famous in privateering a generation later), claiming they had suffered great losses and hoping to make good some small part of the same. The names of those who bought shares in the *Lucy* crop up again and again in the records of privateering at Liverpool: Tinkham, Freeman, Bradford, and Collins. She sailed with "twenty-three officers and men, three owners, a boy, and a cripple." A cripple? Not, perhaps, as odd as it sounds. He was likely the captain's clerk, keeping the accounts, for the captains of such ships weren't always master mariners and in some cases might even be illiterate.

The most oft-quoted incident of the war on the coast of Nova Scotia (perhaps because it showed the Americans in such a good light) was the rescue at Seal Island, fifteen miles off the extreme southwestern tip of Nova Scotia, of the crew of the British warship HMS *Blonde*. The rock on which she floundered, still known as the Blonde Reef, is one of a group of nasty shoals that make the area dangerous for shipping. A sea was running and she quickly broke up, but all her crew, along with sixty-five prisoners captured from American privateers, reached Seal Island safely, losing all their boats in the heavy surf during the landing. And there they might have remained, trying to subsist on the herd of grey seals (a few of which still bred there, though commercial seal hunters had all but exterminated them) had not two American privateers happened along in the nick of time. These were the *Lively* of Salem, under Captain Daniel Adams, and the *Scammel* of Boston, under Captain Noah Stoddard.

Stoddard was all for leaving the stranded English sailors where they were, but Adams sent his boat ashore with a flag of truce and made a deal with the *Blonde* crew, offering to take them off if they would first throw all their weapons into Brig Rock Pond. He proposed to land them at Yarmouth under a flag of cartel. From there they would eventually get a ship to Halifax. Some writers have given Stoddard credit for the rescue — a gross injustice. What really happened was that he sailed back to Salem and raised such a fuss that the local people greeted Adams as a traitor when he arrived, jeering him through the streets, and harassing his family so much that he finally took them to Halifax, sought British protection, and eventually entered the government service, though as a civilian not a combatant.

In Yarmouth, the British naval brig *Observer* took about half the *Blonde's* crew on board and was approaching Halifax when she was overtaken by the American privateer *Saucy Jack*. Thinking the small brig an easy prize, the *Saucy Jack* came alongside, grappled, and was promptly boarded by a huge force of naval ratings and marines. Down came her flag, and the *Observer* escorted her into Halifax as a prize.

In the late years of the eighteenth century the farms of the Annapolis Valley were thriving on trade with the military forts at Halifax, and by the time war broke out wealthy merchant houses at Windsor and Annapolis Royal were shipping out potatoes, apples, meat, fish, and lumber in their own vessels and bringing back bales of cloth, lamps, clocks, chandeliers, china, and silverware for the local trade. The war interrupted the equally lucrative traffic they had enjoyed with Boston, but the hungry maw of the military machine more than made up for the loss: they were enjoying a war boom.

The landowners in the valley were not struggling pioneers but a substantial yeomanry, with valuable possessions in money, jewellery, and silver plate. Some of them were judges, members of the Legislative Council or members of the Provincial Parliament. They supposed themselves safe from surprise attack. They were not, after all, living on the coast, and the coast, in any case, scarcely provided a landing place for raiders anywhere between the Annapolis Basin, which was strongly fortified, and the less strongly fortified Basin of Minas. In addition to the forts there was a supposedly well-organized militia, with muskets, uniforms, and colonels strategically placed and ready to summon them out at the first boom of a cannon. Most of the colonels were retired officers from the regular army, experienced in mustering and managing troops. There was one militia colonel at Wilmot and another at Annapolis Royal.

But none of this stopped Samuel Hall, perhaps the most notorious of all the American "pirates." He moored his sloop *Mary Jane* in an unoccupied cove on the Fundy shore opposite the Gaspereau Valley in the summer of 1778, led his raiders over North Mountain, hid them in the woods, and descended at night on the slumbering hamlets and isolated farms. Hall could not carry off barrels of apples or bales of cloth, for which he would need horses or ox carts. Instead he specialized in more portable goods and is credited with stealing a treasure's worth of jewellery and money from landowners' chests, silverware from their sideboards, and small, well-made items of porcelain. What's more, his raiders got safely back to their ship, which had been left in a dangerous position on an open coast with no safe anchorage. But they never made it out of the Bay of Fundy. A British frigate caught the *Mary Jane* a day or two after the raid.

Hall is one of the few privateers thought to have left behind buried treasure. His loot vanished, the British captain reporting that he'd found no strongbox in the cabin of the

Mary Jane. Perhaps Hall had buried it ashore. That wouldn't have been difficult because he undoubtedly had the help of local sympathizers and guides. There were no shortage of those in Nova Scotia in 1778, many of them dispossessed Acadians who had returned to their homeland after being stripped of their property and banished in 1755. There have been a number of unsuccessful searches for Hall's treasure, even as recently as the mid-years of the twentieth century. But then Hall may not have left any treasure behind. Perhaps he recovered it. Or perhaps it vanished in other ways. Naval captains in the eighteenth century sometimes managed to convert treasure to their own use — treasure that under the articles of war they should have turned over to the Crown for distribution. The idea of restoring it to its owners seems never to have been considered. Once you lost your property to a pirate or privateer it was regarded as salvage. The King was supposed to get half of it, the captain a quarter, and his officers and crew smaller shares according to their rank.

During the war other landing parties from rebel privateers attacked many small Nova Scotia towns. Barrington, Canso, Chester, and Yarmouth were all invaded briefly. Sometimes the local militia put up a stout defence, sometimes not.

At 3 a.m. on September 13, 1780, Simeon Perkins, a prominent merchant in Liverpool, Nova Scotia, was awakened by his neighbour Snow Parker with the shocking news that the rebels had landed in Liverpool Bay, captured the small fort at the mouth of the harbour, and taken the British pickets prisoner. Perkins hurried his son off to rouse the militia officers and alarm the town, then took his spyglass to the nearest hill just as dawn began to break. He saw two small schooners and concluded that the rebels were scarcely

an overwhelming force. Perhaps they could be stopped by
a show of resistance. Perkins and his son and three other
men posted themselves on the road from Fort Point, where
the privateers would have to pass on their way to sack the
town. There was a brief exchange of gunfire, and the privateersmen fled, leaving their leader, Captain Benjamin Cole,
a prisoner in Perkins's hands. Meanwhile the militia had
mustered and was prepared to storm the fort.

Perkins was now able to bargain with Cole, who had no
idea that he was the sole prisoner. All prisoners would be
released, Perkins told him, if the privateers released the
captured soldiers and left the harbour peacefully. Otherwise
the whole landing party would be surrounded, taken prisoner, and shipped off to Halifax. The bluff worked. Cole's
second-in-command agreed to the terms, released the
soldiers, and reboarded the ships. The militiamen and the
regulars kept their side of the bargain too and did not fire
on the vessels as they sailed away.

The best-remembered raid of the war was a piece of
unbelievable daring by American privateers, carried out
with the help of a spy who knew the local conditions, the
state of military preparedness, and the lay of the land. In
the dark hours before dawn, August 28, 1781, a merchant
named John Roach was awakened by men loudly arguing
in front of his house on St. George Street near the centre
of Annapolis Royal. He opened a window to find himself
facing a musket and two men demanding admission to his
house. When he came down to open the door his neighbour came rushing in with the news, "The damned rebels
are in the town!"

In the dark of the night two privateer schooners, one

armed with twelve carriage guns, the other with ten, had sneaked through Digby Gap (where a guard was supposed to be stationed to give the alarm on the approach of hostile ships) and upstream through the waters of Annapolis Basin and past the fort on Goat Island and the Scotch Fort on Granville shore. They had landed right in the town under the guns of Fort Anne.

The schooners had a guide with them, an Acadian who had been convicted of petty theft at Annapolis Royal two or three years earlier and had been branded on the right hand — a common sentence in those days. According to law, the red-hot iron was to be withdrawn after the victim had screamed out "God save the King" three times.[1] The man who guided the Americans up the basin and into the fort at Annapolis Royal was said to be seeking out the sheriff who had passed sentence, with the idea of killing him. Perhaps the reference is to John Ritchie, justice of the peace and judge of the Court of Common Pleas, who had been appointed in 1778 and who was taken prisoner by the American raiders. There was no sheriff at Annapolis Royal until 1782. In any case the Acadian guide led the Americans into Fort Anne without opposition. The fort seems to have been unoccupied that night, even by sentries. But in the darkness the Americans mistook their guide for a sentry and shot him dead. He was the only casualty of the whole affair.

The militia rolls for 1776 show 103 men at Annapolis Royal, under the command of Colonel William Shaw, but none of them put up any show of resistance that night. All three forts seem to have been standing empty. One historian says three men from the regular army were assigned to guard Fort Anne, but if so they were drunk, asleep, or absent. Not a shot was fired, except for the one that killed the Acadian guide. The Americans had planned their raid carefully, had good advance intelligence, and carried it off almost without a hitch. One by one they roused the townsmen from sleep and paraded them at gunpoint into the "moat" — a dry ditch surrounding the fort — with an armed guard standing over them. Women and children were allowed to remain at home.

By daylight the privateers were rampaging freely through the town, looting the merchants' stores and any private house that looked worthy of their attention. They had spiked the guns in the forts[2] so that their two armed ships, with forty crewmen left on board, had undisputed command of the basin. Requisitioning carts and horses to carry booty down to the King's wharf, the raiders spent the day loading their vessels with everything movable, not only store merchandise and household valuables but even the contents of private pantries and wardrobes, leaving many of the people with nothing to eat and nothing except the clothes on their backs — probably little enough of that too since many of them had been turned out in the middle of the night. Women were allowed to keep the shoes they were wearing but had the silver buckles cut off and carried away as contraband of war. One woman lying ill (said to be Mrs. John Ritchie, wife of the justice of the peace) sent her black slave-woman to the wharf where the privateers were loading the loot to appeal to them for mercy. They sent the slave back with her apron full of sugar, tea, and biscuits.

Among the loot removed from the merchants' stores were puncheons of rum, which the privateers opened on the spot and consumed in great quantity. Fortunately the privateer captains had sufficient control of their men to keep the drunken party from degenerating into a riot. No man was beaten. No woman was raped. No house was burned. In the afternoon, on hearing a rumour that the militia was mustering in the valley, the privateers departed hastily, taking with them as prisoners Thomas Williams, the leading magistrate, and John Ritchie. Both were soon released on parole in exchange for American prisoners at Halifax. Ritchie was elected to the Provincial Parliament the following year.

This bold attack on what was supposed to be one of the most strongly fortified places in Nova Scotia should surely have convinced the British of the need to garrison the outports. But it didn't. Their sole interest seemed to centre on Halifax, where they organized invasions of all the rebellious states from Maine to the Carolinas. And so, when the Americans undertook a privateering raid against Lunenburg on July 1782, they again landed almost unopposed. This new settlement, founded by German immigrants under a British plan of colonization in 1753, was situated specifically for defence on a narrow peninsula sixty miles west of Halifax by road (even then there was a road of sorts, passable by mounted riders if not by carriages) or forty miles by sea. The town was difficult to approach without a pilot, even from Lunenburg Bay, and it was almost impossible for ships to approach from Mahone Bay, on the other side, though small boats could come and go by this route.

In 1782 Lunenberg was defended on the east, toward the sea, by a blockhouse and on the west by two forts overlooking the town, with shore batteries that should have been able to defend it from any attack by sea. There were also picket lines for defending musketmen and barracks for troops. As at Annapolis Royal all these defences were empty when the Americans arrived at dawn, having landed just before daylight at Blue Rock Cove near Red Head, three miles east of the town.

Five privateer ships, manned by crews of 150, armed with forty-four cannon, and accompanied by a "rowing galley" (possibly a large landing craft), had put ninety men ashore at Red Head. Magdalena Schwartz, out to milk her cow, discovered them marching towards the town and ran to warn her husband, who ran in turn to alert the defenders. The Americans fired at him, but he escaped unhurt, and the noise of musket fire awakened the slumbering inhabitants. John Creighton, formerly a British army officer, was colonel of militia, his house close by the eastern blockhouse. Hastily summoning five neighbours with muskets, he took command of the blockhouse and began firing at the approaching raiders.

Meanwhile the ships had left their anchorage and sailed around East Head into the inner harbour, where they landed another party of men with four ships' guns. This party then rushed up the hill behind the town, took over the forts, spiked the twenty-four-pounder shore batteries that could have sunk their ships on approach, and rolled the guns off their mountings, downhill almost to sea level.

Other crewmen had hauled their ships' cannon up to the deserted forts and trained them on the town. They now controlled both Lunenburg and the approaches to it by sea. Colonel Creighton and the other defenders in the eastern blockhouse were outflanked and under the attackers' cannon. Their musket fire had wounded three or four of the invaders but to no purpose. They had no choice but to surrender.

The Americans clapped Creighton into irons and placed him
prisoner on board their flagship, the *Scammel*, commanded
by Captain Noah Stoddard of Boston. Stoddard apparently
planned and directed the whole operation, and like the raiders who sacked Annapolis Royal, he obviously had detailed
information concerning the exact state of the town's defences.

The privateers now proceeded to sack the town, or as
the *Boston Gazette* gleefully expressed it, they "fell to plundering with a natural and pleasing vivacity." Indeed there
was an element of playfulness in their actions, but there was
serious purpose too: they confiscated guns and ammunition
wherever they found them. Barrels of gunpowder and tubs
of cannon balls intended to supply the forts were removed
to the ships' holds. They looted the stores of everything.
They seemed to be especially fond of the scarlet uniforms
supplied for the militia. Soon they formed a parade, some
dressed in the scarlet uniforms, others in bows, laces, and
plumed bonnets. The "vivacious" visitors tossed all kinds
of merchandise about the streets and looted the shops of
supplies of cakes, raisins, and figs, which they generously
distributed to barefoot boys who gleefully followed them as
though they were a gang of Pied Pipers.

The carnival atmosphere lasted most of the day, helped
along once again by the vast supplies of rum discovered in
the merchants' storehouses: no fewer than twenty puncheons
— not mere casks, mind you, a puncheon was an oversized
barrel made of oak, holding as much as a hundred imperial
gallons, not of the watered stuff sold today but of proof
spirit. The war had made good rum a scarce commodity
in the rebel colonies, and this was the world's best, straight
from the British Caribbean.

The privateersmen trussed up a local Protestant clergy-man, the Reverend Johann Gottlob Schmeissar, who made a nuisance of himself trying to stop the looting, and left him lying in the street, but apart from that and the arrest of the militia leaders, they behaved rather well: nobody was shot, beaten, or raped. Even the black slaves, who surely might have been confiscated as valuable property, were allowed to go free.

Meanwhile people who had fled from town at the first alarm were trying to get help. Two men started for Halifax in a boat by way of Mahone Bay, but somebody else made it over the "road" on horseback ahead of them, and by noon naval ships had left Halifax for Lunenburg — four or five hours' brisk sailing if they had a fair wind.

A mere seven miles overland from Lunenberg to the southwest, at LaHave Ferry, Major Joseph Pernette, a militia officer, received word of the raid around noon from refugees who had escaped the town. He would have started his march by seven or eight o'clock in the morning had there been cannon fire from the town, but there was none. He signalled the local militia by firing off a cannon, collected twenty men, and started off, leaving word that others were to follow as soon as they were mustered. It took more than three hours to cover the seven miles through woods and marshes; he arrived at 4 p.m. and joined Major Jessen, at the head of another small party of militiamen, on a hill behind the town. At this point the Americans sent a messenger to the gathering troops with word that they would put the whole town to the torch if the militiamen approached any nearer. To emphasize their threat, they set fire to the large house belonging to Colonel Creighton near the eastern blockhouse. It went up in flames, but the fire did not spread into the town.

Having taken everything of value, the Americans got the local merchants together and demanded a ransom. The Americans suspected that quite a lot of money might have been hidden in the first few minutes of the raid. So the three leading men of the town not under arrest signed a promissory note for £1,000 in favour of Captain Stoddard, payable at Halifax within thirty days. There seems to be no record that the note was ever redeemed, but it very well might have been because the war was virtually over. More than eight months before the raid on Lunenburg, General Charles Cornwallis had surrendered a British army of more than seven thousand men at Yorktown in Virginia, ending the fighting on land. Though Cornwallis had not been defeated in the field and had lost only a handful of men, he was starved into surrender, largely by the outstanding success of the American privateers, who had captured and confiscated numerous shiploads of supplies, including vast amounts of arms, powder, and shot, intended for the British forces. It is said that the only bayonets possessed by General George Washington's army were captured from British ships.

The other factor that brought the war in America to an end was the French navy and a strong expeditionary force of French troops. France sent no fewer than twenty-eight ships of the line to blockade Chesapeake Bay in 1781 and had eight more on the way when a British force of nineteen ships of the line attacked and was defeated. The French fleet involved in this battle was almost as large as the one assembled at Trafalgar twenty-four years later.

Even after the fighting on land had stopped, the war at sea continued. But the British fleet had departed from the American coast, and in 1782 the American privateers were having a glorious romp up and down the Atlantic seaboard, collecting all the loot they could lay hands on before the peace treaty put a stop to it. Meanwhile the British and French fleets were battling for control of the West Indies. The British, French, and Americans signed preliminary articles of peace on November 30, 1782, four months after the Lunenburg raid. Privateering against the Atlantic colonies ceased, though the worldwide naval struggle between Britain and France continued for another seven months, with the final shots fired in the Indian Ocean in June 1783.

The Americans had made such an enormous success of privateering during their War of Independence that it filled them with confidence and plunged them into the disastrous War of 1812. It had taught the Maritimers, and especially their merchants, a lesson they wouldn't forget. Soon, taking advantage of the wars of Napoleon, they would be reaping the rewards of legalized piracy along with the Spanish Main, while their relatives in New England chewed their nails and cursed the stagnation of their foreign trade.

1. There were also many sentences of flogging at Annapolis Royal, all served upon Acadians, who formed the landless labouring class. They were also sometimes sentenced to serve as bond-servants to the merchants whose property they had stolen.

2. A soldier spiked a gun by driving a metal plug into its touch hole with a mall. The plug was then sawed off flush with the gun metal so it could not be withdrawn. The only way to restore the gun to service was to drill out the plug with hand tools.

CHAPTER 10
GODFREY AND
THE *ROVER*

L IVERPOOL, NOVA SCOTIA, is a quiet little town
on the estuary of the Mersey River, eighty-seven
miles by road southwest of Halifax. It lies at the
inner end of a narrow bay that widens suddenly to seaward,
with Coffin Island at its centre. The Mersey, which comes
pouring out of the great inland lakes, widens into a snug
harbour at the point where it meets the sea. There a wide
pool, less than a square mile in area, forms what the French
call a barachois, its entrance guarded by small islands and
rocks. To the south of the barachois is Fort Point, with its
docks and its historic marker, a reminder of the days when
Liverpool fought Napoleon and his allies, the Dutch and
the Spaniards, and then a few years later battled the greedy

Americans, who tried to take Nova Scotia away from the King of England.

Founded in 1760 by emigrant New Englanders, Liverpool was at first just a fishing settlement, but the settlers soon discovered the huge pines and spruces of the inland plateau and began milling logs that floated down from the virgin forests on the waters of the Mersey River. The best of the white pine became ships' masts, not only for the local trade but also for export to distant shipyards in New England and Europe. The rest was shipped as squared timbers or milled into lumber locally. Besides its safe harbour and access to the back country, the little settlement had another advantage. It lay halfway between Halifax, its main supply base, and Cape Sable, where ships turned the corner into the Bay of Fundy and the Gulf of Maine. It was well located for trade, peaceful or otherwise, with New England.

But none of this explains why in the closing years of the eighteenth century and the early years of the nineteenth, when warfare was an almost constant way of life and private warships sometimes tipped the scales in the balance of power between great nations, this little town became the privateering capital of British North America, filled with ambitious young shipowners who made their fame and fortune "in the cannon's mouth." Liverpool's success as a privateering centre came largely from the breed of men who lived there, men who built up a tradition not only of seamanship, of long-range navigation and trading, but also of daring, of taking real risks with their lives and their money. Some of them lost, but others gained both great prestige and great wealth. An aristocracy of risk-takers, a club of men who gambled with life and wealth, met regularly around the tables of the counting houses in Liverpool, while their agents recruited venturesome sailors in waterfront taverns such as the Widow West's (later, the Widow Dexter's).

The earliest privateer from Liverpool of which we have a record was the *Lucy*. She served against the Americans in the War of Independence, with no particular distinction, but some of the people who owned and manned her became famous privateersmen, especially her principal owner, Simeon Perkins, and her captain, Joseph Freeman.

A contemporary of the *Lucy*, the *Resolution*, under Captain Thomas Ross, a Loyalist who had escaped to Canada, fought one of the bloodiest battles in the history of privateering. On July 10, 1780, the *Resolution* met the American privateer *Viper* off Sambro Light, Halifax. The two ships pounded each other with cannon fire for about an hour and a half, until both were badly damaged. In the end the *Resolution* surrendered, with eighteen men dead. But the *Viper* had fared even worse, with thirty-three killed. It was rare indeed that such carnage would occur between privateers: a loss of fifty-one lives in a single battle was virtually unheard of.

The armed merchant ship *Isabella*, attacked in the same war by the American privateer *General Sullivan* (fourteen guns and a crew of 135 men), fought the privateer for two hours "yardarm to yardarm" before the privateer pulled away "in a sinking condition." On her return to Liverpool the *Isabella* reported her losses: two men killed outright, one other who died of an amputated leg, three with disabling wounds (loss of hand, a shattered knee, etc.), and six or seven with slight wounds. The ship had taken 132 cannon shots in the hull and rigging. The "sinking" *General Sullivan* actually limped into port without her mainmast.

She had lost eleven of her crew, a heavy loss of life by privateering standards.

Simeon Perkins was justice of the peace for Liverpool, a colonel in the militia, and eventually a member of the Legislative Assembly of Nova Scotia. He had made a fair bit of money out of the American War of Independence, and when the Napoleonic Wars reached the Caribbean Sea, with Spanish ships fighting on Napoleon's side, he built a large ship especially designed for privateering: the *Charles Mary Wentworth*. She was fitted with sixteen cannon, making her nearly the equal of a sloop-of-war, and carried a crew of sixty-seven men and four boys, under Captain Joseph Freeman, the man who had commanded the *Lucy*.

The *Charles Mary Wentworth*'s first prize was auctioned at Halifax for £7,460. Her second brought £1,110. In two cruises she took five ships for a total return of £19,000. Then on her third cruise she drew a blank because of illness among her crew. With such success behind him, Perkins decided to go whole hog and fit out his vessel like a fully commissioned warship. He shipped eighty-two crewmen (eleven of whom were boys between the ages of twelve and fifteen), including a company of ten marines under a sergeant and a master-at-arms. The crew drilled constantly in gunnery and in hand-to-hand fighting. But it all went for nothing. No valuable prizes fell to the *Charles Mary Wentworth* on her fourth voyage. No hard battles were fought. The cruise was a financial failure, and the cost of maintaining the ship was so great that Perkins decided to lay her up, content with his earlier winnings.

Just as she was laid up, another newly built ship took her place. Perkins held a share in that one too, the *Rover*. Her captain was Alex Godfrey, and her first mate was a young man later to become the most famous privateersmen and the wealthiest shipowner in Nova Scotia, Enos Collins. She sailed to the Caribbean and returned in less than a month with three valuable prizes, one with her holds full of Madeira wine and another carrying eleven hundred barrels of sperm oil. On his second voyage in the *Rover* Godfrey showered himself with glory, turned a handsome profit, and won the lasting love of an erstwhile enemy. The voyage has become a Maritime legend, and many of the details are recorded in an account that Godfrey wrote on his return.

Failing to meet any worthwhile prizes on the high seas, the *Rover* headed for the coast of Venezuela and began harrying the Spanish coastal shipping. She had done so much damage on her first voyage and was now making such a nuisance of herself that the Spanish governor of Puerto Cabello decided to fit out a small squadron to capture her. He armed three gunboats and a large schooner and sent out a smaller coastal schooner as bait. The small schooner was instructed to lure the *Rover* close to harbour, where the armed ships could pounce on her. Godfrey sailed straight into the trap. He was quickly overtaking the trading schooner when the *Santa Rita* came out of Puerto Cabello, armed with two twelve-pounders, ten six-pounders, a hundred sailors, and twenty-five marines. The wind was so light that sails were almost useless, and the *Santa Rita* was towed by two of the gunboats, each carrying a six-pound gun and thirty marines. The gunboats were rowed by black slaves chained to the benches and driven by whips. A third gunboat, identically armed, tried to manoeuvre to cut off the *Rover*'s escape to seaward.

The force arrayed against the little hundred-ton privateer was overwhelming, and Godfrey sent his nephew Henry to the powder magazine to blow up the ship if she should be captured by the Spaniards. "Fall into the hands of God, not into the hands of Spain," Sir Richard Grenville was reported to have said in a similar situation some two centuries earlier. In 1800 Spain still had a bad reputation for torturing and murdering prisoners. Against 215 fighting men, including 115 marines, Godfrey could muster only thirty-eight men and fourteen guns — all of them four-pounders. But he had one advantage. The *Rover* was light, and though the wind was of little help on that day, she could be swung about with the aid of long sweeps worked from the deck. Quickly swinging his vessel at right angles to the *Santa Rita*, he fired the seven guns on that side directly into her deck at point-blank range.

Then spinning through a quarter turn, he brought the seven guns on his other side to bear on the gunboats, hitting one with three guns and the other with four. Chaos broke out on the two slave galleys, and the third beat a hasty retreat. Godfrey then turned his attention back to the *Santa Rita*, his four-pound guns already reloaded and ready for action. He took time to notice that dead and wounded slaves from the two shattered galleys were being thrown into the sea by the marines.

The two schooners then began exchanging broadsides. According to Godfrey, the action lasted for three glasses, a "glass" being a sand-timer that ran for half an hour. Then the wind came up, and the *Rover* began to make for the open sea. Suddenly, to everyone's surprise, they heard a loud crack from the *Santa Rita*, and her foretopmast fell in a heap of spars and ropes across her bow. She was temporarily out of control, and Godfrey decided to seize his opportunity. He put his headsails aback, swinging his stern close to the rail of the temporarily disabled ship, and led a boarding charge to the deck of the Spaniard. It was a bold move, but it paid off. Fifty-four men lay dead or dying on the *Santa Rita's* deck. The only surviving officer was the young lieutenant of marines. Without leaders the sailors and marines alike fled below decks.

The ship's flag still flew at the masthead. She had not formally surrendered. But at this point a young lad came running from below, ran up the rigging, toes clutching ropes till he reached the truck and cut away the flag with his knife. It fell into the sea. Then he slid down the ropes to the deck and threw himself at Godfrey's feet, begging for his life. Godfrey prudently took the boy's knife, then reached down and stroked his head reassuringly. He was a compassionate man, with children of his own, and this waif who feared for his life touched his heart at once. He probably knew no Spanish, but he managed to reassure the boy. In any case he soon discovered that he had a small shadow: the young Spaniard attached himself to the victorious captain and refused to be regarded as a prisoner of war.

The *Rover* returned from her voyage to such a reception in Liverpool as few small ships of war have ever enjoyed. She had two prize ships, including the large *Santa Rita*, and hundreds of prisoners, who were sent to Halifax to be held for exchange when the opportunity came. Within a few months, they had all gone free. Simeon Perkins recorded the arrival of the *Rover*, accompanied by the *Santa Rita*, in his diary. Five days later her second prize, the *Nuestra*

Señora del Carmen, sailed in with the prize master Lodowick Harrington and a crew of ten. They had nearly starved on the voyage and had put in to Cape Cod for supplies. At auction the two prize ships brought a total of £1,078. Alex Godfrey bought both ships and graduated from privateer captain to merchant-shipowner.

The young Spaniard who had surrendered the *Santa Rita* isn't mentioned in the documents, but he lives on in the oral tradition of the town of Liverpool, where it is said that he refused to be repatriated with the other prisoners and became instead a member of Godfrey's family. In time he too was a trader and shipowner. Indeed he may well have been one of the Liverpool privateersmen who served with such conspicuous success against the Americans a few years later.

The ships of Godfrey's time hadn't made much advance over the ships sailed by the Kirkes more than a century and a half before. Merchant ships were still large, beamy tubs, with as much hold space as possible. There had been some improvement in sail plan but not much. Warships had narrower, faster hulls and were no longer top-heavy with armour, a design flaw that had caused more than one of them to capsize and sink in harbour in the eighteenth century. But all ships were still built by shipwrights who had learned their trade and their designs from fathers and grandfathers. The day of innovative designing, the day of the clipper, was still a generation away.

Guns had improved in range and power, but when mounted on a ship were not very accurate, even within half a mile. They were much more effective when mounted on stone foundations ashore and that was why shore batteries were so dreaded, even by the most powerful warships. The

warship was less a fighting machine than a means of trans-
porting armed men from place to place. Captures depended
on overtaking your victim until you lay within speaking
distance, with the threat of grapeshot or boarding or both
if she failed to surrender. Time after time the rigging of
the two ships was actually entangled before the duel was
decided. But all this was slowly changing. Even then the
shipyards on Chesapeake Bay in Maryland were beginning to build something called the Baltimore clipper, not
a clipper as we understand it, not a true greyhound of the
sea, like the famous *Flying Cloud* or *Cutty Sark* but moving
in that direction. And by the time the next war loomed,
this design had evolved far enough to make the small, fast
privateer a more effective instrument of war than it had
ever been before.

CHAPTER 11
MASTERLESS MEN

VISITORS TO NEWFOUNDLAND'S Southern Shore — that picturesque strip of coastline that runs almost due south from St. John's to Cape Race — will see as they drive from Ferryland to Cappahayden a prominent spur of rock rising to a height of almost one thousand feet some five or six miles inland. This is the Southern Butter Pot, formerly the lookout point and eastern boundary of the territory ruled by the Masterless Men.

Various prominent hills in Newfoundland are called the Butter Pot, the best known of which is in Butter Pot Provincial Park, overlooking the town of Holyrood and the waters of Conception Bay. The *southern* Butter Pot overlooks a wild stretch of Atlantic Ocean and the coastline where such pirates as Peter Easton, Captain Jacob Everson, the man known only as Lewis, and heaven only knows how many others, found haven.

Behind the Butter Pot lies a stretch of caribou barrens, woodlands, and bogs running southward and westward to St. Mary's Bay and Placentia Bay. A herd of between one and two thousand woodland caribou is found there today.

As many as five or six thousand of the same animals may have roamed those barrens in the closing years of the eighteenth century when the Masterless Men lived there under the leadership of an Irish deserter from the Royal Navy named Peter Kerrivan.

The term "masterless men" goes back at least to the reign of King Henry VIII of England, who signed into law Acts of Parliament dealing with beggars and vagrants. One such act decreed that any person "having no land, master, nor using any lawful merchandise, craft or mystery" should be taken to the nearest market town and there be tied naked to the end of a cart and beaten with whips throughout the same market town till his body be bloody by reason of such whipping. Masterless Men were vagrants and potential outlaws who, after being suitably scourged, were sent back to the town where they were born or where they had last spent three successive years, there to be hired out to labour "as decent men ought."

In Newfoundland a "masterless man" was a fishing apprentice or seasonal labourer who had run away from a planter or English fishing master or else a deserter from the Royal Navy who had escaped from the floggings, starvation, and scurvy that were still the lot of men serving before the mast — "scum of the ports" as their officers called them, swept up by press gangs, shanghaied, and working as slaves in all but name on His Majesty's ships of war.

At the end of the eighteenth century when Napoleon was ravaging Europe, Ferryland was a fortified town and a major centre of the fishery. A century and a half earlier it had been the seat of the first royal governor of Newfoundland, Sir David Kirke. In Kerrivan's time, the 1790s and the early 1800s, it had magistrates, a courthouse of some kind, and, in addition to its shore batteries on the cliffs and on the fortified Isle aux Bois, its harbour usually held a British warship.

Those who had sinned by deed or by neglect against the harsh laws of the time were brought to Ferryland to be tried and punished. The flogging of naked men at the cart tail had been replaced in the reign of Elizabeth by less scandalous if no less brutal forms of punishment at the whipping post and the pillory. The little town of Ferryland had three whipping posts set up along its waterfront, one at either end of the harbour and one at the centre. A servant who had wronged his master or committed some other minor crime such as stealing a gallon of rum would be taken to each place in turn to receive a dozen or more lashes with the cat-o'-nine-tails. More serious crimes were punished with hanging or deportation, that is to say, with temporary or permanent enslavement to a plantation owner in Virginia or, later, in Australia.

There were strict laws regarding servants in the fishery. Every fishing master was responsible for the men he employed and had the power to dock their wages, pay debts on their behalf, hire them out to others, and work them up to twenty hours a day. Every shipowner or captain who brought men from England or Ireland to serve in the fishery was responsible to see that he took the same number of men when he returned in the autumn. If not, he was liable to a fine of ten pounds for each missing head that he could not account for. The object of this law was to prevent "masterless men" from running loose in the colony. But the law was not very effective and was probably not often enforced. Ten pounds was still a lot of money in those times, equal to a man's seasonal earnings in the fishery provided he was industrious, prudent, and lucky. Most fishing servants ended the summer with far less than ten pounds. After the cost of their food and their daily ration of rum was deducted, they might have a few shillings coming, or they might not — the chance that any of them could buy his independence with as much as ten pounds was rather remote. If they simply left their stations to seek their fortunes in the colonies, they would be in debt to the captain who brought them out — and debt was a serious offence in those times. Small wonder that some of them ran off to live by their wits or by petty crime.

It was against this background that the Masterless Men of the Butter Pot Barrens emerged. We know very little about Peter Kerrivan, the leader and organizer of the band, except that he was from Ireland originally, that he was young, and that he was a wily outlaw who managed to evade the best efforts of the British authorities to capture him. He was probably a born leader with a gift for organization because, in a colony where the same conditions prevailed along many hundreds of miles of coastline, this was the only place where the Masterless Men formed a community and left some mark on history.

Near the Butter Pot they built an inland settlement of sorts — a shacktown — from which they ranged inland and up and down the coast, living partly by hunting and partly by plunder.

The Oral History of Ferryland, recorded by Howard Morry of that town and by John Hawkins of nearby Cape Broyle in the 1950s, has much to say about the Masterless Men. They were, according to Morry and Hawkins, "country men" who had learned to live and hunt like aboriginals. The caribou herd was their staff of life. They lived mainly on meat and learned to dress deerskins and used them for clothing almost exclusively. They were semi-nomadic, following the deer, but this would not involve long journeys, for the Avalon herd had little space in which to "migrate." Its seasonal wanderings would cover no more than fifty miles or so.

One or two Mi'kmaq people may have been associated with the Masterless Men. By their time the native Beothuk inhabitants of Newfoundland were nearly extinct, and the few remaining were hiding out in the most remote parts of the island where they would soon be sought out by white men and murdered. They had been replaced by Mi'kmaqs from Nova Scotia, an aboriginal tribe that was better able to deal with Europeans. The Mi'kmaqs lived mainly in the central and south part of the island, but some of them ranged over all parts of the 42,000 square miles of Newfoundland, including the Avalon Peninsula. According to *The Oral History of Ferryland*, Robert Carter, the most prominent landowner of the Ferryland settlement, shot and killed an aboriginal in the hills above Ferryland, and it would seem that the aboriginal in question must have been Mi'kmaq because by that date there were no Beothuks anywhere in eastern Newfoundland.

The Masterless Men traded surreptitiously with settlers in out-of-the-way fishing villages, exchanging meat and hides, and probably furs as well, for such supposed essentials as flour, molasses, and rum. If they couldn't get these "essentials" in any other way, they stole them from the fishing rooms where they also took nets, cordage, guns, and ammunition — things that they found difficult to obtain by trade.

Naturally, this set the merchants and fishing masters against them, and these pillars of respectability complained to the colonial authorities, who in turn complained to the Navy, the only effective law-enforcement agency in Newfoundland at the time. Since the Masterless Men included deserters from the Royal Navy, the navy itself had a stake in bringing them to "justice" — that is to say, in capturing them and stringing them up to a yardarm as an example to any others who might be tempted to choose a life of hardship and freedom rather than a life of hardship and slavery.

Kerrivan's Masterless Men were, in a sense, Newfoundland's first road builders. They were the first Europeans to live in the interior where coastal waters could not provide them with transport, and they had chosen a place where no rivers of any size provided canoe routes. So they cut and improved trails paralleling the coastline far enough inland to be on high, relatively dry ground. They also cut trails right across the interior of the Avalon Peninsula to St. Mary's Bay and Placentia Bay, throwing rough bridges across streams and building corduroy duckwalks over peat bogs. Kerrivan, however, was nobody's fool. He knew that even the roughest road could lead the British Navy straight to his door. So some of the most promising-looking roads built by the Masterless Men were false trails leading into a morass of bogland and there petering out to nothing.

It was a wise precaution. The Navy sent at least three expeditions into the interior to try to round up the Masterless Men and bring them to Ferryland for hanging. These expeditions accomplished little. They found and burned at least some of the shacks at the Butter Pot, not once, but repeatedly. The shacks, however, were empty of men and chattels when they arrived. Everything that could be moved had disappeared into the woods, for the Butter Pot was an excellent lookout from which to see a troop of marines marching inland from the coast.

The shacks were easy to rebuild. The expeditions got lost in the bogs. At least twice they returned empty-handed. But once they returned with two (some accounts say four) prisoners — most likely young recruits to the band recently run off from the ships or the fishing stations and not yet wise to the ways of the woods. The marines never did catch up with their principal quarry, Kerrivan himself, or the main body of his followers. They had to be content with hanging the two (or four) outlaws who had fallen into their hands.

Howard Morry reported that his grandmother, then a child of perhaps five, was taken by her mother from their home in the village of Aquaforte to Ferryland to see the outlaws hanging from the yardarm of the naval frigate where, presumably, their bodies were left for some time "as an example to evil doers." Such examples were expected to impress small children with the wages of sin, and the sight must, indeed, have impressed the child in question because she remembered it and described it to her grandchildren some seventy years later. The date of the hanging seems to have been 1810 or thereabouts.

After that, so far as we know, the Masterless Men were

left in peace by the British authorities, and perhaps they also became more cautious, but in any case they continued to live in the backwoods and to trade with (or prey upon) the plantations until the War of 1812 gave anyone who wanted it all the employment, adventure, and opportunity for quick riches he could desire. Those who shrank from serving in the regiments of "fencibles," who went from Newfoundland and Nova Scotia to do battle with the Yankees, could always get berths on the privateers — licensed pirates who were authorized to prey on American merchant shipping and to keep the loot they captured. During the war whole fleets of them from both sides ranged up and down the Atlantic seaboard, north and south through the Gulf of St. Lawrence, and even to the coast of Labrador.

Some of the Masterless Men were certainly absorbed by the War of 1812 in which Newfoundland took a very active part, while others became respectable settlers. By 1818 or 1820 they had disappeared. As social conditions began to improve, as settlement was encouraged rather than discouraged as it had been formerly, it became possible for the Masterless Men to move quietly back to the coast — not to St. John's or Ferryland or Placentia or any other centre of law and order, perhaps, but to little outports where there were no resident magistrates or police. There they took up the occupation, just then becoming respectable, of independent fishermen.

By the 1820s or 1830s it was possible for a poor man without property to live as an independent settler, no longer needing to be bound to a fishing master to prove his legitimacy but owning his own small house and boat and making his living with his own hands. By that date a "squatter" could even build a house on Crown land if it was otherwise unoccupied and after a generation or so could legally claim it as his own simply by virtue of long occupation. This was doubtless what happened to most of the Masterless Men. As social conditions changed, they simply melted into the population of the more remote fishing outports where their descendants are still living today.

Their roads remained behind them and continued in use. When the Newfoundland government instituted regular postal service in the reign of Victoria, the mail was taken on foot from St. John's by postal carriers who travelled routes of approximately fifty miles out and back, their mail sacks on their backs, handing over the sacks at designated points to other carriers and receiving return mail to be delivered on their route. The carriers who operated from St. John's to Cape Race along the Southern Shore, delivering mail to such places as Bay Bulls, Cape Broyle, Ferryland, and Cappahayden, travelled over roads cut out of the bush by the Masterless Men. Their roads overland to the western bays disappeared, but the roads they opened parallel to the shore remained in use until they were replaced by a branch railway line early in the twentieth century and, later, by a modern highway.

Between the two American wars, the War of Independence and the War of 1812, the British North American colonies were in a state of great turmoil and sharply divided loyalty. Much of their trade with America was illegal. Many of the merchants had business connections along the American seaboard and depended on three-way trade between Canada, the United States, and the West Indies — trade that, according to British law, was the monopoly of British firms. It was all very confusing and adding to the confusion was the feeling among at least half the population of English Canada that their eventual destiny lay with republican America rather than with far-off monarchist England.

Out of this turmoil emerged two of the later pirate captains of the east coast, one of them the most successful native-born Canadian pirate of all time, the other a pirate of no real distinction except the negative distinction of being the last man hanged for piracy in Canada.

Samuel Nelson was a Prince Edward Islander, born somewhere around the time of the American War of Independence. His father, John Nelson, was a prosperous landowner who received his first grant of Crown land "for cultivation and for pasture" near Charlottetown on September 5, 1796. By 1805, when Samuel Nelson married, the family had become so well-to-do that his father was able to give him a farm as a wedding present. He also received a commission in the militia, but neither farming nor soldiering particularly appealed to him. He had a taste for trade and for the sea. He bought a brig and set up as a small merchant trading to Halifax.

The Nova Scotia capital was at that time an important military fortress, the strongest and best-garrisoned British post in the world outside Great Britain, and a major consumer of agricultural products. Nelson flourished for a time as a merchant trading between Prince Edward Island and Halifax. Then he fell into some kind of disgrace, said to be a scandalous sexual adventure, and lost his commission. He left his wife, now the mother of several children, at home in Prince Edward Island and went off to live in Halifax, where he received a new commission as a lieutenant in the Nova Scotia Fencibles.

In Halifax he met a retired privateer named Morrison who believed that there might be opportunities to exploit the trade with the former American colonies, especially because of their willingness to accept cargoes from British colonial possessions without demanding strict accounting as to their origin. Morrison had the knowledge and the experience of the privateering trade. Nelson had the money to finance a voyage. They formed a partnership and bought an American sloop mounting ten guns.

From the Nova Scotia fishing fleet they recruited a crew of some ninety men willing to risk their necks for a fast buck and began their piracies by capturing a trading brig inward bound with a cargo from Europe. They then sailed the brig to New York, posing as shipowners and traders, and sold both ship and cargo at a fair price.

With this comfortable start and a good supply of powder and shot, they next sailed to the West Indies, where they began raiding both the shipping and the plantations. In the West Indies Nelson and his crew acted with great ruthlessness and barbarity. They are reported to have tortured and killed the officers of captured ships and to have murdered both planters and slaves during their raids on the smaller, undefended islands.

Fortunately, although the islands were not defended by forts, there were British sloops-of-war cruising among them. Nelson soon had these pirate-hunters hot on his heels. He fled northward along the Gulf Stream and escaped to the American ports, again paying a visit to New York to dispose of his loot.

After that Nelson and Morrison made a division of the

spoils and paid off many of their crewmen, but their piracies were by no means at an end. Sailing northward with a small crew in their ten-gun sloop, they raised the south coast of Newfoundland where they captured ten fishing ships, recruited more crewmen, and replenished their supplies. Some of the captured ships they released. Others they sent to New York for sale.

Wealthy, and perhaps thinking of retiring while they had the chance, Nelson and Morrison sailed to Prince Edward Island, where Nelson was reunited with his estranged wife. But while coasting the shore of his native island, he ran his ship aground in foul weather. Morrison and some of the crewmen were drowned, but Nelson got safely ashore and rejoined his family.

At that point, if not before, he decided to retire from piracy. He now had a fortune estimated at 150,000 pounds (several million dollars in today's funds). He sold his farm and took his family to New York, where he set up as a legitimate merchant trader.

That was the end of Captain Nelson's connection with Prince Edward Island, but other members of his family remained prominent there. Another Samuel Nelson, possibly the son of the retired pirate, bought land there in 1817, apparently from an older member of the family named John (possibly his grandfather), and remained prominent in land transactions until 1851.

A second John Nelson, probably a younger brother of the pirate, married there in 1815 and had three sons and five daughters whose descendants are living today both in Prince Edward Island and in the United States. There is a tradition in the family that this John Nelson became a sea captain engaged in trade to the Far East, and that he was eventually lost at sea in a passage around Cape Horn.

Edward Jordan, the pirate from Gaspé, had been an Irish rebel before immigrating to Canada. In 1797 he was among the leaders who were secretly training volunteers for the "rebellion of '98." He was caught drilling a company of pikemen at night, tried for treason, and sentenced to death by the English.

Before the execution could be carried out, he escaped and rejoined the rebels. After the failure of the rebellion the following year, the government of Great Britain offered an amnesty to those who would surrender their arms. Jordan took advantage of this and later went to eastern Canada by way of New York and Montreal, acquiring a wife, Margaret, on the way. The family settled at Gaspé, where Edward Jordan served as a fishing shareman with a merchant from St. John's, Newfoundland. After five years' service he had accumulated enough money to begin building his own ship.

In June of 1808, Jordan began trading with the Halifax firm of J. and J. Tremain, and in September of that year they extended him sufficient credit to permit him to complete and outfit the schooner which he then had on the stocks at Gaspé. As security, they took a mortgage on the ship.

In July of 1809 he was in Halifax again, with his schooner, the *Three Sisters* (named for his three younger children). There he was arrested for debt, but his merchant suppliers paid off what was owing and sent him back to Gaspé to collect a cargo of fish. No longer trusting him, however, they sent Captain John Stairs to supervise the transaction and to take possession of the vessel if Jordan should prove unable to pay off the mortgage.

According to Stairs, Jordan had promised the merchants one thousand quintals (approximately 51,000 kilos) of dried fish but was able to deliver only a hundred or so — not nearly enough to clear his debt. Stairs took possession of the ship in the name of J. and J. Tremain and collected from the surrounding fishing rooms a cargo of some 600 quintals. Then he sailed for Halifax with Jordan and his family as passengers.

The *Three Sisters* was a 45-foot schooner with a very high stern and a very wide beam. Jordan must have been very fond of his ship and very proud of her. He had painted her in striking colours of black, white, and yellow. Losing her to the merchants must have been a crushing blow.

Besides Captain John Stairs, there were four crewmen on the voyage from Gaspé to Halifax. The mate was an Irishman named John Kelly. The seamen were Benjamin Matthews and Thomas Heath. With Edward and Margaret Jordan were their nine-year-old son and their three younger daughters.

Shortly before noon on September 13, 1809, the *Three Sisters* was about four miles off shore between Cape Canso and White Head, on course for Halifax. The whole Jordan family was on deck and the mate, John Kelly, was at the tiller. Captain Stairs went below with crewman Thomas Heath and was consulting a book or a chart when he saw a shadow cross the skylight. Looking up he saw Jordan pointing a pistol at him. He jumped as the pistol fired. The bullet grazed his cheek and lodged in Heath's chest.

"My God, I'm killed!" Heath cried, falling to the floor. Stairs rushed to his sea chest where he kept a brace of pistols but found the lock broken and the pistols gone. Overhead he heard several more shots. It was Jordan killing Matthews, the other sailor.

Stairs rushed up the companionway and met Jordan on the top step brandishing a pistol in one hand and an axe in the other. Stairs's rush carried the two of them out on deck, and as Stairs was trying to wrestle the weapons away from Jordan, the pistol snapped without going off. It was a misfire. Stairs wrenched the gun from Jordan's hand and threw it over the side. Almost incredibly, the unarmed captain managed to get the axe away from Jordan as well. But just then Margaret Jordan rushed up with a boathook and joined the fray. Captain Stairs rushed forward, followed by the two Jordans, Margaret with the boathook and Edward with another axe. Seeing a loose hatch cover, he threw it overboard and dived after it, caught it, and hung on.

There was a strong wind and the ship was making fast time. Captain Stairs was quickly left in her wake, and Jordan rushed aft, planning to take the second pistol from Kelly, who was still at the tiller, and finish the captain off. But Kelly persuaded him that Stairs was sure to drown anyway, so they kept on course until they could trim the sails, then bore away eastward.

At about 3:30 that afternoon an American fishing schooner, the *Eliza* under Captain Levi Stoddard, fished Captain Stairs out of the water "almost lifeless" and took him to Hingham, Massachusetts, the *Eliza*'s home port. From there Stairs went to Boston, saw the British consul, and had an alarm sent out for Jordan's arrest. The governor at Halifax offered a reward of one hundred pounds for the pirate's capture.

Meanwhile, Jordan, assisted by his wife and Kelly, sailed the *Three Sisters* into Fortune Bay on Newfoundland's south coast and dropped anchor at Little Bay West, a tiny fishing hamlet in a well-hidden cove a few miles from the important fishing settlement of Harbour Breton.

Here they attempted to enlist two fishermen, William Crew and John Pigot, but the men were suspicious of the odd-looking schooner carrying as crew only two men, a woman, and four small children. They also noted the missing hatch cover and the cargo of fish that was not stowed as it should be for a foreign voyage. They refused to sign on.

At this point John Kelly went ashore, located a magistrate (presumably at Harbour Breton), and told him of his pressing need for seamen. The magistrate called in Pigot, who was unemployed, and threatened to have him tied up and flogged if he refused to join the ship — all this according to Pigot's sworn testimony given later at the trial.

Under duress Pigot joined the ship. They then rounded the Burin Peninsula, crossed Placentia Bay, and ran into St. Mary's, where they attempted to recruit more seamen, without success. They then rounded Cape Race and began calling at ports along the Southern Shore between Cape Race and St. John's, looking for a qualified deep-sea navigator and giving out the information that they were preparing to make a voyage to Ireland.

They found a qualified man named John Power and signed him on for eleven pounds a month — a high wage indeed for a navigator in 1809, at least twice the going rate. Along the Southern Shore they also signed on four sailors, making a total of six crewmen recruited in Newfoundland.

Meanwhile, Mrs. Jordan had been sharing her favours between her husband and the mate, Kelly, and this led to a fight in which Kelly tried to shoot Jordan but was prevented by the navigator, Power. Kelly then stole a boat and rowed ashore where he disappeared.

Finally the *Three Sisters* sailed for Ireland, but she was only about one hour offshore when she was challenged by the Canadian coastguard ship *Cuttle*, which had been sent along the Newfoundland coast with the specific mission of finding her and arresting the three pirates, Edward and Margaret Jordan and John Kelly.

Believing Stairs to be dead, Jordan tried to bluff it out, saying he was blown off course while bound for Halifax, but the *Cuttle* took everyone on board the *Three Sisters* to Halifax as prisoners and sailed the ship into port with a prize crew.

The Newfoundlanders were quickly cleared of blame and released, but the two Jordans, man and wife, were put on trial for piracy. It was a full-dress vice-admiralty trial presided over by the governor, with the captains of naval vessels at the Halifax station as judges.

Margaret Jordan was pardoned, but Edward Jordan was hanged in chains on the Halifax waterfront. Finally, in a storm his skeleton blew to pieces and was washed into the sea. Many years later his skull was picked up at the tide line and was preserved in the Halifax museum.

John Kelly was arrested in Newfoundland, tried, convicted, and sentenced to death, but afterwards pardoned — perhaps because he'd had no actual hand in the murders, although he had certainly aided and abetted Jordan's piracy.

A charitable fund was started in Halifax for Margaret Jordan and her four small children, and eventually they took passage for Ireland.

Although Jordan was the last Canadian hanged for piracy, four other men, all guilty of piracy, were hanged for murder at Halifax thirty-five years later. The series of events began in October 1843 when Captain George Fielding and his fourteen-year-old son George Jr. sailed from Liverpool, Nova Scotia, in the *Vitula* for ports in South America. Fielding's ship was seized and sold for smuggling by the government of Peru, and he and his son got passage on the *Saladin*, bound for London.

With several members of the *Saladin's* crew, Fielding hatched a plot to kill the captain and take over the ship. They carried out the plan, murdering six men altogether, and Fielding took command of the vessel, but he and his son were murdered in their turn by the conspirators.

The six surviving crewmen knew nothing about navigation and, after beating about the Atlantic for some weeks, they ran the ship ashore, with all sails set, on an island off the coast of Nova Scotia. They were arrested and taken to Halifax for trial. The whole story of the *Saladin* murders was that of a sordid, drunken brawl, scarcely deserving to be called piracy. In fact, the survivors were not accused of piracy, but of murder. Nevertheless, the press made a great issue of the "*Saladin* Pirates." Two of them turned Queen's evidence and were reprieved. Four of them were convicted and were hanged together on Halifax Commons, creating a great sensation. The date of the hanging was July 30, 1844.

CHAPTER 12
THE *BLACK JOKE*

THE SINISTER-LOOKING LITTLE SHIP swung at her anchor in Halifax Harbour. Built in the United States, bearing a name proudly worn by a long succession of pirate vessels, she had been caught running slaves from Africa, condemned under British piracy laws, and was up for sale. She had been used as a tender to larger slave-carriers rather than as a principal in the illegal trade. Even though slaves were practically stacked like cordwood, the *Black Joke* was too small to handle more than a few score of them at a time.

The only buyer who showed much interest in the ship was a young merchant from Liverpool who had recently opened an office in Halifax. Enos Collins, an impeccable gentleman in a beaver hat, with walking stick and gloves, was no mere small-town shopkeeper. Able and ambitious, he was an experienced seaman who had trodden decks in all weathers and served as first mate on the famous fighting ship *Charles Mary Wentworth*. Collins had returned to Liverpool with enough money to set himself up as a shipowner and trader. But in ten years his small fortune had only grown slowly. He was about to invest a major part of it in a gamble with two Liverpool partners, but like every successful gambler he was close-mouthed about what he was doing. If it paid off, he had every intention of founding an international trading company — perhaps even a dynasty.

The shrewd merchants who crowded the dock looking for bargains among the ships that had been condemned by the Vice-Admiralty Court and ordered to be sold to enrich the King's coffers must have wondered about Collins's interest in the *Black Joke*. She hardly met their standards for a money-maker. Never designed for bulk cargo, speed and manoeuvrability were her only advantages, and those didn't earn many pounds or dollars in 1811. The little ship was a mere fifty-three feet overall and an inch less than nineteen feet on the beam. There was little more than headroom in her hold — six and a half feet. She was registered at sixty-seven tons. Technically a Baltimore clipper, she was two-masted and schooner-rigged, but that did little to describe her. In addition to fore and aft sails on both masts, she carried square sails on her foremast, giving her some of the advantages of both schooner and square-rigger. The most freakish-looking thing was the angle at which her masts were stepped. If her pictures are to be credited, they were raked aft at twelve degrees or more, giving her the predatory look of a pirate vessel. She also had an exaggerated bowsprit that jutted far forward like the snout of a wolverine and carried three big headsails. Her sail plan and dimensions would make the *Black Joke* a poor performer in bad weather, but good for racing, tacking, and coming about, especially in light or moderate winds.

Collins must have had special plans for this ship. A yacht? But he was not yet in the class who indulged in fifty-three-foot pleasure boats. She would make a good gun-runner, but there was no current demand for such a trade. Perhaps he meant to sell her overseas. The other merchants lost interest in their speculations and let Collins have his way. He bought the *Black Joke* at the rooms of the Spread Eagle tavern for the sum of £440, not exactly a steal but a good bargain. He sailed her home to Liverpool on November 10, 1811, without telling anyone about his long-range hopes for the ship. All he would say was "I'll use her as a packet for fast runs up and down the coast." She could, indeed, carry a few passengers and mail, but you'd never get rich in that trade. Collins's secret plan was undoubtedly something quite different.

Speed and manoeuvrability, Collins knew, gave a small warship the advantage she needed to capture enemy merchant vessels and run away from enemy cruisers. At the moment there was no demand for private warships in North America, but that might change overnight. Napoleon was still loose in Europe. The Americans were making threatening noises. It was true that Admiral Horatio Nelson had established British command of the seas, but it was not likely to go unchallenged for long. Meanwhile Collins would use his speedy little ship as a courier. That way she'd earn her keep while waiting for her big chance. He renamed her the *Liverpool Packet* and applied for the mail contract. She carried her first packages on the initial run from Halifax to Liverpool.

On June 18, 1812, with disputes over maritime trade and impressment of American sailors for an excuse, the American Congress declared war on Great Britain. Britain was fully occupied in Europe, and Napoleon had been encouraging the hawks in Congress to seize what looked like a golden opportunity to push the American border north to the Arctic Ocean. Taking over the continent north of Mexico would be "a mere matter of marching."

It was a time when most Americans believed that the remaining British colonies in North America were itching to throw off the yoke of England as they had done, to join with them in the glorious dream of life, liberty, and the pursuit of dollars. Besides, they believed it was the manifest destiny of the United States to unite the whole continent under a single flag and a single economic system centred in New York.

The New England merchants did not share this dream. Trade, not territorial expansion, was their interest, and the war would play havoc with their trade. They not only opposed the war but also continued secretly trading with the enemy. A strange and confusing situation! While their vessels sneaked up the coast as far as St. John, buying and selling goods that might well have been classed as war supplies, other vessels from the same ports sailed out, armed to the teeth, to capture the trading ships of New Brunswick and Nova Scotia.

The war had been going on for nine days before news of it reached Halifax. Then HMS *Belvidera*, a sixty-four-gun cruiser, arrived with the dead and wounded, and prizes of war. She had been attacked by three American warships but had escaped and captured three American trading vessels.

Collins and his partners decided at once to convert the *Liverpool Packet* to a privateer. But there was a long delay while they waited for a letter of marque. The governor of Nova Scotia considered such a matter beyond his authority and sent the request off to Great Britain. The British waffled, confident in their sea power. Why share prizes of war with private corporations? When they finally issued the letter of marque, they failed to specify American ships as prizes and made Collins and company put up a bond of £1,500 against disputed seizures. Meanwhile the *Liverpool Packet* was commissioned to sail to Boston under a flag of truce carrying civilian prisoners taken from an American ship by the Navy. Such prisoner exchanges continued to be frequent throughout the war.

When she returned to Halifax, she was outfitted as a privateer with "five rusty cannons that had been serving as gate posts on the waterfront." Rust or no rust, they were heavy armament. One was a twelve-pounder and the others six-pounders,[1] big stuff for a ship of her size. Four-pound carriage guns would have been normal armament for a tiny sloop-of-war like the *Black Joke*, but the twelve-pound shot, with its ability to smash through decks and hulls and bring down masts and rigging, served her well over the next three years. By the time Collins had added muskets and pikes, grappling irons for boarding, leg irons and handcuffs for prisoners, she was one of the deadliest little craft afloat.

The War of 1812 was the final flowering of privateering. Privateers had been vital to the American War of Independence, when the fledgling nation had issued letters of marque to no fewer than 515 ships and had captured 1,345 ships flying the British flag, most of them from the colonies of Newfoundland, Nova Scotia, and the West Indies. The Americans confidently expected to repeat their success in this new war. "If it floats, arm it!" cried the hawks in Congress as they issued letters of marque even to whaleboats and single-masted shallops, which could mount nothing larger than a single small swivel gun without danger of sinking themselves.

In Nova Scotia it wasn't quite so easy. The British were reluctant to allow colonial governors to wage war. They demanded high bonds of indemnity from privateering corporations. The naval commanders were opposed to privateering altogether. If an auxiliary fleet were needed, they felt the ships should be commandeered and commissioned under the direct orders of the naval commanders. This, however, would have cost a great deal, and in the end wealthy shipowners were allowed to wage war for private gain.

Commissioned as privateers, Collins and company next had to strengthen the decks of their ships to withstand cannon fire and fit bulwarks with ports for the guns. Below decks they had to build steel-clad and, with luck, fireproof powder magazines and shot lockers. Then there had to be quarters for crews ten times the normal size. Extra men were needed not just to man the guns or to board ships that put up a fight, but as prize crews to sail captured ships into port. The glittering prospect of a share in prize money made it easy to get volunteers to fight the War of 1812. Doctors, lawyers, and clerks abandoned their offices. In Newfoundland the outlaws known as Masterless Men flocked to the ports and enlisted. Even a few clergymen left their pulpits to seek their fortunes on the Great Deep. There was no age limit. Any boy big enough to tote a bucket was welcome as a "powder monkey" and might expect half a man's share of the spoils. Better by far than going to school or serving as apprentice to a brick-maker.

Collins and his *Black Joke*, tangled in red tape, were slow off the mark. Not so the Yankees. By the end of July 1812 an estimated 150 American privateers were scouring the Atlantic coast. Perhaps the most famous of them was the *Yankee*, a Rhode Islander that made six raids northward into Canada and eastward into the Atlantic, capturing forty prizes reputed to be worth $5,000,000.

The great braggart Thomas Boyle of Baltimore was also active in the early months of the war. Many of his exploits were certainly imaginary, but it is equally certain that he made a great nuisance of himself. He commanded a fast clipper that was able to snatch prizes from armed convoys, even in Britain's home waters.

It was up to Collins and his partners to redress the balance. They fitted out a whole fleet of privateers, but the little *Black Joke* was the deadliest of the lot. Bristling with arms and crewed by seasoned men, she finally left Liverpool on August 30, 1812, and headed for Cape Cod. She was not the first Canadian privateer at sea. The *General Smyth*, sailing out of St. John, had taken her first prize on August 13, and in cruises lasting ten weeks captured prizes worth £7,119.[2]

It wasn't just the ship, of course. The man who commanded the *Black Joke* during the first year of the War of 1812 deserves to be as well known to Canadians as John Paul Jones is to Americans. Captain Joseph Barss was a dashing young man in fashionably long hair and sideburns, lean and dark, with the look of an Elizabethan and the character of a Drake or Hawkins. His record as commander of a single fighting ship was rarely equalled, even by the great pirates of the eighteenth century. In October 1812 Barss took eleven vessels in one week off Cape Cod; then, in a single day, made prizes of nine fishing schooners with cargo valued at $50,000. All this was reported with indignation in the Boston and Salem newspapers. Where, they demanded, was the navy of the Republic? Why was it unable to deal with this one small ship? Barss, still hovering off Massachusetts Bay, found himself with such an embarrassment of riches that he began releasing all but the most important prize ships (after confiscating any portable valuables) and saving his crews to man the larger ones. Only five of his biggest victims reached the Vice-Admiralty Court in Halifax that month.

He then sailed home for a refit and more crew members, but was back off Cape Cod by December 10, where, according to the *Boston Messenger*, he captured eight or nine vessels, valued at from $70,000 to $90,000, within twenty days of the time he left Liverpool. The Boston editors fumed. This mere scrap of a warship was running a virtual blockade on the doorstep of America's largest port. They demanded that a fleet be sent out to capture her. They urged immediate work on a canal to bypass Cape Cod — a work actually completed a hundred years later.

Barss and his crew spent a triumphant Christmas with Collins and his partners in Liverpool. Twenty-one ships that they had captured were moored in the Mersey River within sight of the town. After all claims were settled and the Crown deducted its share, the prize money came to over $100,000 (equivalent to about $2,000,000 today) — not bad for three and a half months' work.

In February and March of 1813 Barss sent thirty-three prize ships to Liverpool. But the luck of this great sea rover was running out. On June 11, with most of her men sailing for home in captured ships and only thirty-three hands on board, the *Black Joke* chased a large American schooner, which turned out to be a privateer far more heavily armed and far more strongly manned than she. As the American turned to give battle, the *Black Joke* ran for her life. Barss moved his best gun, the twelve-pounder, to the stern and threw all the others overboard to lighten the ship. But in the stiff wind the bigger ship had the advantage and slowly gained. Barss fired off every twelve-pound shot in his locker without stopping his pursuer. At last, with nothing left to fire and the American still overtaking him, he hauled down his colours. In spite of the fact that the *Black Joke* had already surrendered, the Americans swarmed on board with muskets blazing and killed four of the crewmen before the two captains could stop the fray. They were the only men lost in the battle.

It was a great day for Portsmouth, New Hampshire, when the schooner *Thomas* brought the terror of the seas into harbour, a little wasp of a ship that had captured more than a hundred American vessels and sent some fifty of them to auction. Chivalry on both sides was typical of the naval war of 1812. British and Americans went out of their way to rescue enemy sailors and treated them decently. Prisoner exchanges went on all the time. But Barss and his crew had humiliated too many New England seamen. A mob lined the streets to jeer at the prisoners as they were paraded in irons through Portsmouth. Officials acted no better. They locked Barss into fetters and fed him on hardtack and water. When they finally released him in a prisoner exchange, after months in jail, they forced him to sign an affidavit undertaking not to engage again in privateering against American shipping. It was an undertaking he would have to respect, even though made under duress. Should he be captured again in a fight with an American ship, he would probably be hanged as a pirate. And so Barss shipped instead as master of a trading schooner to the West Indies. By a strange coincidence the ship he commanded was the same one that had taken him prisoner. The *Thomas* had been captured by HMS *Nymph*, condemned, and sold at auction.

Barss took no further part in the war, but his famous little ship was back at sea in fighting trim even before his release. She now flew the stars and stripes under yet another name: *Young Teaser's Ghost*. This strange nomenclature arose from the fate of the American privateer *Young Teaser*, herself a successor to the *Teaser*, a small privateer that sailed out of New York in the first months of the war, armed with only two guns and a crew of fifty. When a British cruiser captured her, after five months of privateering, they didn't consider her worth salvaging and burnt her at sea.

The *Teaser's* crew were sent home in a prisoner exchange, her officers on parole. This was a system in which the paroled officer signed a bond not to take part in privateering for a specified period, a year perhaps, or the duration of the war. Officers were supposed to be men of honour, whose parole could be trusted. If they turned out not to be they might be "hanged like dogs."

Among those paroled from the *Teaser* was her captain, Frederick Johnson, who, in violation of his parole, volunteered to sail on the *Teaser*'s successor, *Young Teaser*, a more powerful ship owned by the same privateering firm. This rather remarkable craft was 124 tons, built of oak, sheathed in copper, and painted black, with an alligator figurehead. She was armed with two long guns, one of them on a swivel as a bow-chaser, and three caronades. And she carried a crew of sixty-five. Johnson did not sail as her captain but as lieutenant, or first officer.

The *Young Teaser* made only one voyage. She took two small prizes almost in the mouth of Halifax Harbour on June 9, 1811, and this daring deed was her undoing. She was chased by the *Sir John Sherbrooke*, a powerful Liverpool privateer, and by two small naval vessels, but she escaped from all of them. Then, on June 26, she was cornered by two British warships in Mahone Bay, a short distance southwest of Halifax. First on her tail was the *Orpheus*, a naval frigate that spent the day cruising back and forth to seaward, preventing the privateer's escape from the island-studded waters. In the afternoon the *Orpheus* was joined by *La Hogue*, a seventy-four-gun battleship. The *Young Teaser* kept dodging back and forth among the islands, where the larger ships could not follow her, hoping to escape after dark. But darkness comes late to northern waters at the end of June, and there was still plenty of daylight at 7:30 p.m., when *La Hogue*'s captain dropped anchor and sent off five armed boats, each mounting one gun and loaded with armed men, to attack the privateer. The *Young Teaser* lay becalmed. The attack was timed so that darkness would fall just before the boats reached the privateer — some time after 9 p.m. — making them difficult targets for the *Young Teaser*'s guns. If she decided to fight, her crew would have to man the bulwarks to try to repel boarders, who would be there in overwhelming numbers.

The captain of the *Young Teaser* was still trying to make up his mind whether to haul down his flag when First Officer Johnson went dashing down the companionway to the ship's powder magazine, carrying a "coal of fire." A moment later the deck of the *Young Teaser* blew skyward in a tremendous explosion. Johnson had escaped hanging by blowing himself and the ship and all but eight of his shipmates to eternity. The carnage was dreadful. Floating corpses and parts of corpses drifted ashore for the next two days. The hulk burned right down to the waterline. Captain William Dobson, standing right at the after rail when the ship blew to pieces under his feet, was one of the survivors. What's more, he wasn't taken prisoner. Somehow he got ashore and made his way back to New York, where he received command of the third *Teaser*, the formidable *Black Joke*.

She made just one voyage under her new name and new flag, failing to take a single prize. Her owners, perhaps disgusted by three successive failures, offered her for sale, and she went back to sea under yet another captain and yet another name, the *Portsmouth Packet*. She still had no luck. Sailing north into the Bay of Fundy, she was promptly cornered by a British warship and forced to surrender. In two voyages under the stars and stripes, she had not captured even one ship. Back to the auction block went the old *Black Joke*, her third time in two years, and who should buy her but Enos Collins!

For captain he found a likely young man, a New Brunswicker named Caleb Seely, who had made a reputation sailing out of St. John in the tiny privateer *Star*. Though Seely never equalled the record run up by Barss, he did very well indeed, capturing at least fourteen ships in eleven months. And he may have done much better than this, for some of the records from 1814 have been lost. After a brief and brilliant career in two privateers, Seely retired from the sea, became a shipowner, and founded yet another merchant house at Liverpool.

Another Liverpool seaman, Lewis Knaut, now took command of the *Black Joke* and sailed off on one more privateering voyage in October 1814. By this time the blockade of the American coast was so tight that few prizes remained to be captured. American shipping had been practically driven off the seas. In her last two months as a merchant raider the *Black Joke* took only four ships.

Her final score is uncertain. Incomplete records of the Vice-Admiralty Court confirm that sixty-eight of her prizes went to auction. But there were many others. A great storm at Liverpool wrecked some of the ships waiting there to be taken to Halifax. Because she carried such limited manpower, she burned, sank, or released many of her smaller victims. One hundred and thirty might be a reasonable estimate. All told, she was the most successful merchant raider of the War of 1812 and a vital factor in the blockade that strangled the American economy and preserved the independence of the colonies that would unite, fifty years later, to form the nation of Canada.

Collins? Well, he not only founded a great merchant house but also the Halifax Banking Company in 1825. At the time of his death he was reputed to be the wealthiest man in British North America.

The little *Black Joke* enjoyed certain advantages in addition to her speed and manoeuvrability. Her rig and her deep
keeling allowed her to sail closer to the wind than most of
her rivals. She was painted black and with sails lowered was
inconspicuous against the dark New England shore. Most
of her sails could be handled from the deck and hoisted
quickly the moment a victim appeared. She took her first
two prizes September 7, 1812: the 325-ton *Middlesex*, bound
for Boston with a mixed cargo, and the *Factor*, with a load
of Port wine destined for Providence, Rhode Island. Next
she liberated the *Maria* from Gibraltar, which had been
captured by an American privateer; then, in five days, made
prizes of five American schooners and sent them to Halifax
for auction.

1. Cannons were still classed by the weight of their shot. Heavy guns caused so much
recoil that small ships could not mount and fire them without the danger of loosening
seams and springing planks.

2. Reckoning inflation at twenty to one, this would be well over $500,000 in today's
funds.

CHAPTER 13
WINNERS AND LOSERS
IN THE WAR OF 1812

THE *CROWN*, OUT OF HALIFAX, was the smallest of the Canadian privateers. A forty-foot schooner, called by fishermen a jack-boat, she carried a crew of thirty young desperadoes, most of them under the age of sixteen. It's a nice question how thirty people managed to fit themselves into a forty-foot boat, even if many of them were not full grown. The answer seems to be that they slept on deck under sail canvas, an expedient that must have been common on bigger privateers as well. In addition to muskets and cutlasses, this band of apprentice pirates had a nine-pound cannon that must have shaken their ship from topmast to keel whenever they dared to fire it. With almost unbelievable bravado, this tiny privateer sailed out to do battle with the damn Yankees. And sure enough, back she came with a fat prize: the Boston brigantine *Sibae*, which fetched the magnificent sum of £5,062.

Off she went again, looking for more victims, and reportedly sent in several of them before an American privateer with six guns and a crew of eighty men caught up with her. The *Crown* put up a spirited running fight before she finally surrendered. The Americans admired their young enemies, treated them gallantly, and at the first opportunity sent them back to Halifax in a prisoner exchange.

Many other notable privateers sailed out of Liverpool, Halifax, and St. John's during the War of 1812. The most imposing was the *Sir John Sherbrooke*, named for the governor of Nova Scotia. Largest and best-armed of the Collins fleet, the 278-ton *Sherbrooke* was built especially for privateering and was heavily armed with eighteen guns and a crew of 150 under captain and part-owner Joseph Freeman.

Designed to survive an encounter with any American privateer then afloat, this privately owned warship might have been a dangerous opponent even for a naval sloop or frigate. She brought in nineteen prizes in three months for a profit of approximately $50,000. But in spite of her winnings she proved too expensive to maintain as a privateer and on later voyages began losing money. The Collins corporation then decided to convert her into a merchant ship for the West Indian trade. With a reduced crew and somewhat reduced armament she sailed to Jamaica and the Windward Islands, but luck was still against her. An American cruiser cornered, captured, and burnt her in 1814.

Joseph Freeman had a younger brother, Thomas, who

served as a prize master on the *Black Joke* (along with the other Freemans: Benjamin, Samuel, and Seth.) After sailing many a captured ship into Liverpool, Thomas Freeman had made enough money to enter the ranks of owners and masters, so he bought a share in a ship of the Collins fleet, the seventy-foot topsail schooner *Retaliation*.

This small ship carried five guns, including a twelve-pound long gun, mounted forward on a pivot so that it could be aimed in any direction except due aft. The long gun (classified like other cannon by the weight of its shot) was the most effective weapon of its time because of its greater range and accuracy. Its one drawback was that it burned a tremendous amount of powder every time it was fired. The caronade, the class of gun usually carried by privateers, could fire shot just as heavy as the long gun but had neither the reach nor the accuracy of its big sister. It was, however, much more economical and very effective in the point-blank battles of the time, when ships lay almost rail to rail blasting away at each other.

Thomas Freeman's *Retaliation* was a gold mine. On his first voyage the young captain took four large prizes, so that the corporation cleared approximately $30,000 on an investment of $2,600. Freeman took his winnings and retired from the wars, but his successor, twenty-five-year-old Benjamin Ellenwood, captured nine more American ships valued at over $50,000. Ellenwood then graduated to a larger privateer, the *Shannon*, also owned by a Liverpool corporation, and sent nineteen more ships to the Privateers' Dock at Halifax. By the age of twenty-six Ellenwood was wealthy and passed the command of the *Shannon* to his prize master, John Brown, who captured three more prizes with her before graduating to the *Rover*. Ellenwood did not live to enjoy his plunder, however. Eight months after retiring from the *Shannon*, he was murdered on Dolby's Wharf in Halifax.

The *Rover* of Liverpool was a captured American privateer, renamed in honour of the ship commanded by Alex Godfrey in his famous battle with the Spaniards. On his first cruise Brown captured thirteen ships in three days, then passed her on to Captain Thomas McLaren of Liverpool, who captured five more before the war ended in 1815.

Though Liverpool was the home port of most of the famous Canadian privateers in this war and Halifax the commercial centre of the trade, other ports in what are now the Atlantic provinces took part. In Annapolis Royal a corporation of local merchants, William Bailey, John Burkett, Thomas Ritchie, and John Robinson, put up the money to commission and arm the fifty-ton schooner *Matilda*. John Burkett Jr. sailed as her captain, with a crew drawn from Annapolis, Granville, and Digby. She sent home thirteen prizes in three months before being captured by the Americans, who later sent her under flag of truce to Halifax with prisoners for exchange.

While still in commission as a privateer she was joined by the *Brooke*, purchased at auction by Phineas Lovett, another merchant of Annapolis Royal, with Daniel Wade as captain.[1] She was somewhat undermanned for a privateer, with a crew of thirty-five, but covered herself with glory, snatching prizes from even the very mouths of American shore batteries: seventeen of them in the summer of 1813, when Wade retired and was succeeded by Captain William Smith of Halifax.

They didn't succeed too well. This coast, a crenellated shoreline of islands, bays, and river estuaries, became the favourite prowling ground for a fleet of nasty little boats oddly named "shaving mills." Some of these were surely the smallest warships ever awarded letters of marque. They were often mere whaleboats, propelled by oars, with a dozen armed men out to see what they could seize in the way of legalized loot. For armament they would have, at most, a single swivel gun mounted in the bow, with a barrel of powder and a tub of shot to keep it ready for action. Their speciality consisted of raiding isolated farms and hamlets, and the list of their pathetic plunder has an almost comic ring: sheepskins, kitchenware, men's trousers, women's sewing baskets, children's shoes.

Unfortunately, it was not all comedy. One of these piratical jack-boats, the *Wily Renard* descended on an isolated farm at Sheep Island, New Brunswick, in December 1812, killed a poor settler named Francis Clements, and raped his wife. Captured a few days later, the crew was sent in irons to Halifax, but they were neither prosecuted nor punished for their crimes. They were treated as prisoners of war and released in a prisoner exchange some time later. It was a sad breach of justice, even though the war at sea was generally conducted according to international rules and the "honour of gentlemen."

American privateersmen were as active in this war as they had been in the American War of Independence, and only gradually did the Canadian privateers gain the upper hand. The most far-famed American captain was Thomas Boyle of Baltimore, whose first command, in 1812, was the Baltimore clipper *Comet*, built for the slave trade at a time when every slaver was, by British law, a pirate and fair prey for the Royal Navy. The *Comet*, cross-beamed to allow her to mount heavy armament on deck, carried fourteen guns and a crew of 120. Boyle's success early in the war in capturing ships bigger and better-armed than his own was partly the result of his daring and seamanship, but also because most of his prizes were manned by small peace-time crews of no more than two dozen men and boys, unprepared for warfare and outnumbered as much as five to one.

Many of Boyle's claims to stunning victories against great odds are dismissed by historians as bragging fictions, but enough of them *are* documented to make him one of the leading seamen of his time. On his second voyage he ran into a convoy of two large British merchantmen escorted by a Portuguese man-of-war, heading for Pernambuco, Brazil. Boyle managed to talk the man-of-war out of taking an active part in the battle because the United States was not at war with Portugal. But the Portuguese waffled. Though the warship did not fire on Boyle's privateer, she did fire on his boats when he tried to send out boarding parties. In a night-long cannonade Boyle reduced both merchant ships to mere wrecks and managed to board one of them, but decided she was too badly damaged to be worth capture. In the end he allowed both of them to limp off, still escorted by the warship.

Boyle told this story, with embellishments, to the newspapers and became such a national hero that he was given command of the pride of the Baltimore fleet, the brig *Chasseur*, with sixteen twelve-pound guns and a crew of one hundred men. With this ship he captured many valuable prizes, some of them snatched from convoys under the very noses of the Royal Navy. Convoys were often widely scattered, and their escorts were armed sloops or frigates. Boyle's clipper-built ship, while no match for one of those warships in a gun duel, could outsail most of them. And when not actually in action he could sail under false colours, an accepted stratagem of the time, hoisting the American flag only at the last moment and sometimes gaining the additional advantage of surprise.

In the early months of 1813, Boyle managed to interfere seriously with the supply of the forts at Halifax, while remaining well out of range of its deadly shore batteries. He also plagued shipping bound into the Bay of Fundy, then crossed the Atlantic and plucked prizes right from the English Channel. Not content with this twisting of the Lion's tail, he decided to declare a blockade of the British Isles and sent his proclamation to London in a cartel, as it was called — a ship sailing under flag of truce with prisoners for exchange. The document was directed to Lloyds of London, to be posted, though there is no record that they ever did so. It was couched in the following terms:

> *Whereas it has become customary with the Admirals of Great Britain, commanding small forces on the coast of the United States, particularly with Sir John Borlaise Warren and Sir Alexander Cochrane, to declare all the coast of the said United States in a state of strict and rigorous blockade, without possessing the power to justify such a declaration, or stationing an adequate force to maintain said blockade,*
>
> *I do, therefore, by virtue of the power and authority in me vested (possessing sufficient*

*force), declare all the ports, harbours, bays,
creeks, rivers, inlets, outlets, islands and sea
coast of the United Kingdom of Great Britain
and Ireland in a state of strict and rigorous
blockade.*

*And I do hereby require the respective officers,
whether captains, commanders, or commanding
officers, under my command employed, or to be
employed, on the coasts of England, Ireland and
Scotland, to pay strict attention to the execution
of this my proclamation.*

*And I do hereby caution and forbid the
ships and vessels of all and every nation, in
amity and peace with the United States, from
entering or attempting to enter, or from coming
or attempting to come out of any of the said
ports, harbours, bays, creeks, rivers, inlets,
outlets, islands or sea coast, under any pretence
whatsoever.*

*And that no person may plead ignorance of
this, my proclamation, I have ordered the same
to be made public in England.*

Given under my hand on board the Chasseur,
day and date as above.

Thomas Boyle

Boyle got away with this and subsequent exploits right
through the three years of the war. After he returned to the
western Atlantic, the Royal Navy sent the frigate *Barrosa*
in pursuit of him. She got within sight of the *Chasseur* on
several occasions, and once the chase was close enough to
force Boyle to throw ten of his sixteen caronades over the
side to lighten his ship, but he managed to escape.

Boyle's greatest glory was a battle with an armed schooner that he chased and caught near Havana, February 26, 1815. At 1:26 p.m., within pistol shot of the enemy, the *Chasseur* received a broadside of round, grape, and musket balls. Boyle opened fire, and according to his own account of the battle, "At this time both fires were heavy, severe, and destructive." It was then that Boyle discovered that the schooner was far from the weakly manned vessel he had imagined: "I now found that I had a powerful enemy to contend with, and at 1:40 p.m. gave the order for boarding, which my brave officers and men cheerfully obeyed with unexampled quickness; I instantly put the helm to starboard to lay them on board, and when in the act of boarding she surrendered."

Boyle's prize proved to be His Majesty's schooner *St. Lawrence*, commanded by Lieutenant J.C. Gordon and formerly the famous privateer *Atlas* of Philadelphia. By Boyle's account "a perfect wreck," she reported six men killed and seventeen wounded, several of them mortally. The *Chasseur* suffered five men killed and eight wounded, including Boyle.

But the killing and bloodletting were for nothing. The War of 1812 had been ended by the Treaty of Ghent two months and two days before Boyle's most famous sea duel. Like the Battle of New Orleans, also famous in American song and story and also fought after the war was over, the fighting was all a mistake, caused by the incredible slowness of communications.

American history still credits the United States with winning the War of 1812. Even Canadian historians sometimes describe it as fought to a draw, so a few facts are in order. The Americans did not achieve a single one of the objectives they had set out when the war began. Even the "freedom of commerce and of sailors," which was the excuse for starting the war, was not mentioned in the peace treaty. The repeated invasions of Canada by American armies had all failed. Every American army had been driven back across the border, and American territory was occupied by British troops in various places. The northern half of the State of Maine was occupied by troops from Nova Scotia. But above all, Canadian privateers had won the war at sea. They had outcaptured the Americans by four to one. They had virtually put an end to American maritime commerce, both domestic and international. American exports dropped from $45,000,000 the year before the war to $7,000,000 the year it ended. A few American victories in individual naval duels did much for national glory but nothing for the economy, which, by the end of 1814, was in a state of dire depression, while the economies of Nova Scotia, New Brunswick, and Newfoundland were all bursting with war prosperity.

The War of 1812 was Canada's war of independence, when native Canadians, led by small groups of British regulars, fought off the one major attempt to take their country by force of arms. And without detracting from the victories of the tiny armies along the St. Lawrence and the Great Lakes, it must be said that the privateers, mainly those sailing out of Nova Scotia, were the principal line of defence that prevented Upper and Lower Canada, New Brunswick, and Nova Scotia from becoming American territories and eventually American states.

Newfoundland had taken a smaller part in the war of the

privateers than had Nova Scotia or even New Brunswick. Only two vessels are recorded as sailing on privateering voyages out of St. John's. Nevertheless, at the war's end there were thirty American prize ships moored in the harbour there, and some five hundred American prisoners housed in the military barracks ashore. Newfoundland's trade with New England had always been one of her most important overseas efforts, and as soon as news of the peace treaty was received, the governor began issuing licences for trade with the American states. Eleven of the seventeen licences issued that summer went to former American ships.

Privateering in the War of 1812 was the last great burst of a business that had enriched maritime merchants for centuries. The Americans, who had embraced privateering with such success during the wars against France and in their War of Independence, had learned their lesson and were eager enough to sign international protocols by which privateering was to be outlawed. Naval officers had always despised privateersmen, and by mid-century the professionals had their way. A few privateers fought on both sides in the American Civil War, but their effect was not very great. No letters of marque were issued by Britain in the Crimean War, and it was in 1856, at the end of that conflict, that the first international agreement to outlaw privateering was signed, a ban that has stood the test of time. For though ships that had been privately owned fought in both world wars and one square-rigged sailing yacht became a highly effective merchant raider in the First World War, all such vessels were commissioned as regular elements of the belligerent navies, manned by

naval officers and men. The days when wars were fought
by private enterprise were over.

1 . The ship appears as the *Broke* in most histories, and the captain's name is misspelled
   "Waid". The spellings given here are those appearing in the application for letters
   of marque.

CHAPTER 14
THE PIRATE OF THE THOUSAND ISLANDS

THE NIGHT OF MAY 29, 1838, was rainy and cold as the Canadian steamer *Sir Robert Peel* bound from Brockville to Kingston stopped for firewood at Wells Island in the St. Lawrence River. The Thousand Islands, now a great summer resort filling the upper course of the river where it empties out of Lake Ontario, were then the haunt of bands of brigands whose numbers had been increased by refugees from the recent rebellions in Upper and Lower Canada. When the rebels were crushed by the army, hundreds of them had fled, some with a price on their heads, all of them liable, if caught, to be hanged or transported to the penal colonies in Van Diemen's Land, as the island of Tasmania was then called.

As the *Sir Robert Peel* dropped anchor at Wells Island, a man named Ripley approached the captain and told him he had seen a longboat full of men prowling the narrow waterway as they had approached. Moreover, he had heard a shout, "Here she comes!" The captain laughed at him. He was not afraid, he said, of any gang of ruffians in a boat unless they numbered more than a hundred men.

That was a grave mistake. At two o'clock in the morning, while most of the crew were still ashore and the sixty-five passengers were soundly asleep in their cabins, a band of twenty to twenty-five armed men dressed as aboriginals with painted faces stole out of the woods, boarded the *Sir Robert Peel*, and captured the ship with hardly a show of resistance.

The "Indians" went whooping about the decks with cries of "revenge for the *Caroline*." The captain well understood the import of this war cry. The Canadians had burned the American steamer *Caroline* a few months earlier while she was attempting to land supplies at the rebel base on Navy Island in the Niagara River — one of the centres of the short-lived rebellion led by William Lyon Mackenzie.

The attackers, armed with rifles, pistols, bayonets, swords, and pikes, placed a guard at the gangway to prevent the shore party from coming on board the ship. Then they smashed the cabin doors, hauled the lightly clad men and women out of their berths, and prodded them onto the deck with gun butts and bayonets. The pirates beat several of the men and were about to kill one of them who was wearing the coat of a British officer when the frightened man convinced them that the coat was not his own, so they spared his life and let him off with a beating.

The passengers, terrified, cold, and half-naked, were herded ashore where they took shelter in a log shed along with the stranded crew while the pirates put off in the *Sir Robert Peel* and quickly ran her onto a reef, whether by accident or design is unknown. There they looted the ship at leisure, getting away with the immense haul of $100,000 in cash, the army payroll destined for the troops in Upper Canada, and valuables, including silver plate, money, and jewellery from the cabins valued at another $75,000. As they left, they set the ship on fire. Next morning, by good luck, the stranded passengers and crew were rescued by an American steamer.

The man behind this attack was Bill Johnston, the most notorious of the St. Lawrence River pirates, a self-proclaimed "patriot" of the Canadian rebels who announced that his capture of the ship was an act of war in the struggle to "liberate" Canada. But in fact it was an act of pure brigandage by a man with little interest in politics but a very deep interest in loot. Johnston was a pirate by choice, a rebel only by chance.

He was born at Trois Rivières, Quebec, on February 1, 1782. In 1784 his family settled at Bath, near Kingston, where, as a young man, he was a farmer and merchant. Then like many others living along the border, he extended his merchant interests into the smuggling trade.

Shortly after the outbreak of the War of 1812, the Canadians suspected Johnston of smuggling and of consorting with the enemy. Among other things, he had married an American woman and had many friends and in-laws on the American side of the river. At the same time, he was charged with desertion from the Canadian militia. He was thrown into jail at Kingston, and all his property was confiscated.

Determined not to sit out the war in prison, Johnston escaped and hid in the woods, where he fell in with a band of American fugitives. Six of them stole a large canoe and headed out across Lake Ontario for the American shore. They were picked up by an American ship and landed at Sackett's Harbor, New York.

To their subsequent grief, the Canadians refused to reimburse Johnston for his confiscated property, valued at some fifteen hundred pounds. Burning with hatred for his country and vowing revenge, he offered his services to the Americans.

For the duration of the war Johnston was an enemy spy and raider. Big, strong, fearless, and ruthless, he led a gang of irregulars in a swift six-oared boat, prowling the waterways of the Thousand Islands, which he knew so well from his years as a smuggler. With this small party of raiders he terrorized outlying Canadian farms and hamlets and attacked small craft on the river.

Once his gang robbed a mail coach running between Kingston and Gananoque, leaving the coachman tied to a tree and passengers robbed of their clothing. Another time he ambushed a despatch rider carrying military papers and shot the man's horse, leaving him to complete his journey on foot.

As cunning as he was bold, Johnston eluded all attempts to apprehend him. On one occasion his boat was cast away on the Canadian shore during a gale. All of the gang were captured except Johnston who remained in hiding for two weeks and again managed to make his escape across the lake in a stolen canoe.

At war's end Johnston settled in French Creek (now Clayton), New York, as a merchant. As a traitor he could not, of course, return to Canada without the risk of being hanged. But he spent almost as much time in his former country as in the country of his adoption. French Creek was a notorious smugglers' roost, and Johnston soon became one of the most successful outlaws in the business, using various hideouts among the Thousand Islands on both sides of the border. He swaggered about with six pistols and a Bowie knife tucked in his belt, ready, as he boasted, to take on all comers.

He had various boats at his command, but his favourite vessel was twenty-eight feet long, propelled by twelve oars, and could easily accommodate a band of twenty armed men. Johnston had some of the tastes that marked more famous pirates of an earlier day: he had the hull of his little ship painted black, the sides white with a yellow stripe, and the interior a brilliant red. It was so light that two men could pull it up a slipway and move it overland.

By the mid 1830s Johnston's gang included his sons, John, Decater, James, and Napoleon, and his daughter, Kate. Known to romantics as "The Queen of the Thousand Islands," Kate Johnston was a young woman who could handle a boat as skilfully as any of her brothers. From the Johnstons' base in French Creek she acted as spy and informant for her father and kept him supplied with provisions on those occasions when he had to go into hiding.

In 1838 Upper and Lower Canada (now Ontario and Quebec) were mired in the turmoil that followed the rebellions of 1837. Rebels who had fled across the border to the United States began organizing loosely knit "patriot" groups whose common purpose was the invasion and "liberation" of their homeland. They hoped for aid from the Americans;

actually thousands of Americans joined them. Some were truly sympathetic, believing that America had a mission to liberate the world and that Canada was ripe for revolution. Others were merely drifters and adventurers looking for any booty they might lay their hands on by raiding across the border. Johnston was one of those.

He became a "patriot" when "General" Van Rensselaer created him "Commodore of the Navy in the East" at Navy Island. The "patriots" made attempts to invade Canada along the Niagara River, but these were all thwarted by the incompetence of the invaders as well as by the presence of regular troops and Canadian militia. After the burning of the *Caroline*, the "patriots" were forced to abandon Navy Island.

At that time neither Canada nor the United States had forces stationed along the St. Lawrence River that were capable of flushing the outlaws from their lairs among the Thousand Islands, but American attempts to co-operate in clearing out those robbers' roosts were half-hearted at best. The situation along the Niagara River was much firmer. The situation along the St. Lawrence was chaotic.

In February 1838 Johnston and Van Rensselaer laid plans to attack Kingston and to capture formidable Fort Henry, which had been built by the British and designed to withstand a full-scale attack by an American army. They had a few hundred men armed with rifles and three cannons stolen from American arsenals, but they hoped to accomplish their purpose with the aid of fifth columnists planted inside the town and the fort.

An American schoolteacher named Elizabeth Barnett heard some of the conspirators discussing the plan in French Creek. The courageous woman crossed the frozen

St. Lawrence on foot, then travelled up the Canadian shore to Kingston to warn the garrison.

While the alarmed citizens of Kingston carried their valuables to the fort for safekeeping, the militia was called up, soldiers were stationed at vital posts along the river and in the town, and the garrison at the fort prepared for battle.

Meanwhile, the "patriots" assembled on Hickory Island, but their invasion never materialized. Van Rensselaer, a notorious drunkard, chose this time to go on an extended bender, and as the days passed his cold, hungry followers deserted in twos and threes, drifting back to American settlements for food and shelter. By the time a patrol from the army base at Kingston was ready to investigate Hickory Island, there remained only a handful of shivering stragglers and some sacks of scrap iron, ammunition for the cannons.

Johnston, disgusted with Van Rensselaer, now decided to wage his own kind of guerrilla war against Canada. His first (and only major) undertaking in this "war" was the capture of the *Sir Robert Peel*, an act that drew cries of outrage from all sides. It was so obviously an act of piracy that even some "patriot" leaders were shocked, although they still hoped it might help to spark a new war. Perhaps their greatest outrage was caused by the size of the loot Johnston and his confederates shared out. Nothing else like it fell to the lot of any band of raiders in the "patriot" war.

The government advised angry Canadians not to take reprisals against their American neighbours. Lord Durham, newly arrived from England to straighten out the colonial mess, offered a reward of $1,000 for Johnston's capture. The governor of New York posted another $500 and smaller amounts for known henchmen of Johnston. But many

Americans, including some of the militiamen on the border, sympathized with the "patriots" so that no genuine attempt was made to arrest any of the pirates. A few were apprehended and then released. Johnston, full of bravado after his sensational exploit, issued his own proclamation:

> *To all whom it may concern:*
>
> *I, William Johnston, a native born citizen of Upper Canada, certify that I hold a commission in the Patriot service of Upper Canada as commander-in-chief of the naval forces and flotilla. I commanded the expedition that captured and destroyed the steamer "Sir Robert Peel". The men under my command in that expedition were nearly all natural-born English subjects; the exceptions were volunteers for the expedition. My head-quarters was on an island in the St. Lawrence, without the jurisdiction of the United States, at a place named by me Fort Wallace. I am well acquainted with the boundary line, and know which of the islands do and do not belong to the United States; and in the selection of the island I wished to be positive, and not locate within the jurisdiction of the United States, and had reference to the decision of the Commissioners under the sixth article of the Treaty of Ghent, done at Utica, in the State of New York, 13th June, 1822. I know the number of the island, and by that decision it was British territory. I yet hold possession of that station, and we also occupy a station some twenty or more miles from the boundary line of the United States, in what was Her Majesty's dominions until it was occupied by us. I act under orders. The object of*

*my movements is the independence of Canada. I
am not at war with the commerce or property of
the people of the United States.
Signed, this tenth day of June, in the year of our
Lord one thousand eight hundred and thirty eight.*

WILLIAM JOHNSTON

Following this bold statement, Johnston continued to terror-
ize the Canadian riverfront, attacking vessels and raiding
farms. In two separate raids on Amherst Island he shot and
cut fingers from the hands of farmers who tried to defend
their homes, and in one of his attacks a farm boy was killed.

With a small flotilla of pirate craft following, Johnston
would man the tiller of his own boat, sitting on a bag that
contained the captured flags of the *Sir Robert Peel*. In one
of his bragging statements issued from time to time from
French Creek, he advised any potential attackers to "bring
their own coffins, as he had no time for cabinet making."

Johnston's name inspired fear all along the Canadian
shore. On July 8, Colonel Charles Grey, en route to take
command of a regiment in Upper Canada, wrote to his
father in England, "There was considerable doubt for some
time how far it would be prudent to take the Ladies up for
fear of attack from Bill Johnston."

Lady Durham, also travelling up the St. Lawrence that
month, wrote in a letter to Countess Grey, "Our voyage
by the Thousand Islands has been most prosperous, no
appearance of Pirates or ill-disposed persons, but we heard
afterwards that Bill Johnston, the most dreaded of these
robbers, had been very near us."

While Johnston was holding a Fourth of July celebration

at one of his island strongholds, eighty men from the Canadian and American forces tried to surround his lair. Because the two detachments did not act simultaneously under combined command, Johnston and all but two of his men escaped, leaving behind their famous longboat. The Canadians blamed the failure on the tardiness of the Americans. The Americans accused the Canadians of moving in too soon.

By November 1838, Johnston was involved with a "patriot" lodge called the Hunters, whose members identified each other with secret signs and symbols and swore oaths to "promote republican institutions throughout the world." This band attempted an invasion of Canada by way of Prescott and nearby Fort Wellington. In command were "Major General" John Ward Birge and "Admiral" Bill Johnston.

Thanks to Captain Van Cleve of the American steamer *United States*, the Canadians had advance warning of the invasion. The Hunters had used the *United States* to transport men and munitions to the Thousand Islands. Van Cleve informed the American authorities, and they, in turn, informed the Canadians.

On November 12, two schooners, the *Charlotte of Toronto* and the *Charlotte of Oswego*, headed for Prescott with a force of several hundred armed men. But the invaders were having problems. The two leaders could not agree on a plan of action. Then Birge complained of sickness, which his companions attributed to cowardice, and withdrew from the campaign. Two hundred others subsequently deserted. After Birge withdrew, a Polish revolutionary named Nils Von Schoultz took command of the *Charlotte of Toronto* with about 170 men on board.

Von Schoultz succeeded in docking the ship at Prescott, but while the invaders argued about what to do next, the mooring rope broke and the ship drifted downriver a mile and a half to Windmill Point. The Hunters under Von Schoultz quickly took over the windmill, a six-storey building with thick walls.

Meanwhile Johnston had run his ship aground. The *United States*, seized by the Hunters, steamed out of Ogdensburg to tow the *Charlotte of Oswego* off the mud bank where she was stranded. Later, another steamer, the *Paul Pry*, joined in the effort to float the stranded vessel.

Meanwhile the Canadians, well aware of what was happening, sent troops to surround the windmill and a small warship, the *Experiment*, to bombard the invasion forces from the river. The action that followed, known in the history books as "the Battle of Windmill Point," would have been pure comic opera except for the fact that a few people actually got killed.

The *Experiment* went into action, lobbing shots from her two cannons at the windmill, the *United States*, the *Paul Pry*, and the *Charlotte of Oswego*. An eighteen-pound ball smashed through the wheelhouse of the *United States* and beheaded her pilot. The two steamers then withdrew, and Johnston used a boat to transfer two of the three cannons to Von Schoultz.

At some point Johnston must have been on board the *United States* as her captain later reported that Johnston had wanted to use her to ram "that damn little boat," meaning the *Experiment*.

A few Hunters from Johnston's ship managed to join

those who were digging in on Windmill Point, raising their number to 192. But by next morning all of the vessels used by the invaders had been seized by either the Canadians or the Americans. Some time during the night Johnston, probably realizing the futility of the operation, decamped with thirty of his followers and all the munitions he could lay his hands on.

The stranded invaders in the windmill held out for four days, then surrendered, and eventually Von Schoultz was hanged.

The Americans, accused by the British of aiding piracy, sent Federal troops after Bill Johnston and the others who had been involved in the attempt to capture Prescott. A few days after the battle a search party caught one of Johnston's sons trying to get a boat to his father. Then they tracked the old pirate to a spot near Ogdensburg and cornered him.

Johnston surrendered on condition that he be allowed to give his weapons — six pistols, a twelve-shot rifle, and the ever-present Bowie knife — to his son.

The soldiers took Johnston to Auburn, New York, where "General" John Birge was already in jail. At a preliminary hearing he was acquitted of all charges stemming from the Prescott raid, but United States Marshall N. Garrow insisted that he be held to stand trial for earlier crimes. Before the second trial could be held, however, Johnston escaped, taking Birge with him.

The Americans offered a reward of $200 for his arrest, and within a few days he was caught again. This time he was sent to Albany for trial, where, despite the fact that he was guilty of murder and piracy, he received the astonishing sentence of one year in jail and a fine of $250.

Jail was no great ordeal for Johnston. His daughter, Kate,

was allowed to share his quarters and take care of him. He was given day leave to visit his friends in town. He even attended a performance of a play entitled *Bill Johnston, The Hero of the Lakes*.

Comfortable as prison life was, Johnston made another break after serving only six months. He vanished into the Thousand Islands and next appeared in Washington with a petition for his unconditional pardon signed by a host of friends and sympathizers. President Martin Van Buren refused to have anything to do with it, but his successor, William Henry Harrison, a veteran of the War of 1812, cheerfully signed the document giving the river pirate his freedom.

Johnston returned to French Creek where he was employed at various times as lighthouse keeper, tavern owner, and smuggler. He owned several islands, three of which he named Ball, Shot, and Powder. It was rumoured that on festive occasions the Johnston family would bedeck their persons and their table with the jewellery and the silverware stolen from the *Sir Robert Peel*, but there is no eyewitness testimony to this.

In 1843, at age sixty-one, Johnston boasted that he could row or sail against the best boatmen on the St. Lawrence. When asked if he thought the rebellions of 1837 and his subsequent private war against Canada had accomplished anything, he replied, "Do you call the expenditure of four millions of British cash nothing?" Canada had, indeed, paid heavily for the fifteen hundred pounds taken from Johnston in 1812.

The retired pirate continued to live, unrepentant, at French Creek until he reached the age of eighty-eight. He died there on February 17, 1870.

CHAPTER 15
THE GREY GHOST
OF FUNDY

THE LAST PIRATE of note to operate in Canadian waters was Mogul Mackenzie, commander of the *Kanawha*, a Confederate privateer that preyed on Union shipping during the War Between the States, then disappeared when the war came to an end and was reported as a ghost ship in the Bay of Fundy for several months thereafter. Mackenzie, a wild man with the instincts of a buccaneer born more than a century too late, was feared not only because of his ferocity in battle, but also because he had the reputation of a fiend who would torture or mutilate a prisoner at the slightest provocation.

When innocent merchantmen began reporting, in the early months of 1865, that they had been chased by a pirate ship, sober authorities on shore generally dismissed their reports as mere nervousness. Piracy was supposed to be a thing of the past, surviving only in the Indian Ocean and the China Sea, stamped out in all Christian lands by the power of the State and especially by Britain's Royal Navy, which had run down and captured not only the last of the Atlantic pirates, but also the last of the slave traders a generation earlier. Or so it was believed. It was true that Mackenzie had gone missing, and his ship along with him, but the ship might easily have sunk with all hands after her last battle or, like so many other ships, have simply vanished in a storm.

The reports persisted. And then in May of that year, an American gunboat sighted a sleek grey ship, remarkably like the missing *Kanawha*, off the southern coast of Nova Scotia. The gunboat chased the ship and ordered her to heave-to for identification. She did not heave-to and she hoisted no identifying signals. Instead, she made off at top speed toward the Canadian shore. The waters where the encounter took place were treacherous. Perhaps the American captain was unsure of the coastline. In any case, the ship supposed to be commanded by the former privateer escaped among the channels near Cape Sable, a region of inside passages and long, winding bays where whole fleets might lie undetected.

Later, off the island of Campobello in New Brunswick, a ship that looked like the missing privateer came in sight of a Nova Scotia schooner, altered course, and began to overtake her. A stiff wind was blowing, and the schooner had short-ened sail. Risking damage to his sails or rigging, the captain of the schooner ordered the reefs to be shaken out and the course altered two points to windward, his ship's best sailing position. The schooner was a good sailor and especially fast when sailing on the wind. The pursuing ship also altered course, but now no longer seemed to be gaining, and the trading schooner managed to stay ahead until she reached Portland, Maine, where she put in for protection while the suspected pirate veered off to sea. Again the schooner's captain met mostly incredulity. Perhaps he was a nervous commander? Was he sure the pursuing ship was actually trying to overtake him?

Skepticism vanished a few days later when a whaler put into port with the news that she had found the trading vessel *St. Clare* abandoned in the Bay of Fundy but *still under sail*. The ship's strongbox was missing. There was no sign of her crew. Because she was too short-handed to put a salvage crew on board, the whaler brought the abandoned ship to port under tow, along with a small boat that had been tied to the ship's stern with the name *Kanawha* painted on her planking.

There could be little doubt what had happened. The pirates had departed in the *St. Clare's* longboat, either taking the crew as their prisoners or throwing them overboard. Why they had left the ship under sail was never explained. Perhaps they had departed in great haste when another sail hove in sight.

Shortly after this a trading vessel from Boston arrived at Yarmouth, Nova Scotia, with the news that she had sighted the *Kanawha* heading up the Bay of Fundy in the direction of Saint John. The trader's captain had been close enough to read the name of the pirate ship through his spy glass. This seemed to clinch the matter. The harbour master at Yarmouth took a full statement from the American captain and sent off a report to Halifax, which was then a major British naval station as well as a fortified town.

From Halifax a small warship, HMS *Buzzard*, sailed to Yarmouth and began a hunt for the pirate. After several days of fruitless cruising in Fundy waters, the *Buzzard* arrived in St. Mary's Bay, chased into harbour at Meteghan by one of the violent storms for which Fundy waters are famous. St. Mary's, a bay that opens southward to the Atlantic, is separated from the Bay of Fundy by the long, narrow point of Digby Neck and the islands that lie to the south of it. It seems that the *Kanawha* with the sinister Mogul Mackenzie had been in and out of St. Mary's Bay just ahead of the *Buzzard*.

The night before the arrival of the warship an Acadian homesteader at Meteghan, a fishing port about ten miles from Cape St. Mary and thirty miles north of Yarmouth, was awakened by an eerie wailing from his beach. Gun in hand, he crept down to the shore to investigate, and there he found a naked man, exhausted and almost dead, with his tongue cut out. The man had been mutilated and thrown overboard by the pirates. Whether he had been one of the *Kanawha's* crew or a prisoner was never explained.

The night after the *Buzzard* arrived at Meteghan the wind rose to near hurricane force, and the small warship lay at anchor in the shelter of a long, rocky point, waiting for the storm to blow itself out. Meanwhile the pirate ship had vanished once more into the inner reaches of the Bay of Fundy, a body of water with no natural port along its southern shore from Digby in the southwest all the way to Minas Basin, a distance of nearly a hundred miles.

At the northern end of the Bay of Fundy, near the entrance to Minas Basin, lies Haut Isle, about ten miles from the nearest fishing villages of Ogilvie and Harbourville. It is about the same distance from the tightly enclosed Advocate

Basin lying between the entrance to Minas and the North
Channel of Fundy stretching toward Chignecto.

In earlier times Haut Isle was named by the Acadian
French settlers "Ile aux Morts," the Island of the Dead,
because it was a trap for ships trying to enter either the
north or south channels of the bay and a place from which
wrecked sailors had little chance of escape. The tides there
have a range of almost fifty feet, and the tide race runs like
the current of a great river. The island rises at one point to
a height of 300 feet and is surrounded by cliffs ranging from
80 to 200 feet in height. There is only one landing place, at
the extreme eastern tip and then only at low tide.

The same night that the *Buzzard* was sheltering at
Meteghan, the fishermen along the Nova Scotia shore from
Ogilvie to Harbourville saw rockets exploding in the midst
of the storm and by the glare of sheet lightning could see a
distant ship apparently being swept toward Haut Isle under
bare poles, her sails either furled or blown away. She was
driven by mountainous seas and sucked toward shore in the
tide race. No boat could be launched from the fishing villages, and even if it could, it would be unable to cross the ten
miles of chaos that lay between Haut Isle and the watchers.
The rockets blossomed and died uselessly, and the watchers
saw no more of the ship.

Next day, when the storm died down to a tremendous
ocean swell and fishing boats put out from Harbourville to
search for wreckage or bodies, they could find no trace of
the distressed ship. Every spar, every plank, every drowned
body and scrap of clothing had been swept far out to sea by
the retreating tide.

No trace of the *Kanawha* or of Mogul Mackenzie was

ever found. HMS *Buzzard* called off the search and returned to her station, and it gradually came to be accepted that the sea lanes around southern Nova Scotia were safe once more.

Perhaps not surprisingly, Haut Isle is reputed to be a treasure site. The treasure supposed to have been buried there was not Mackenzie's — his treasure, if he had any, doubtless went down with his ship — but that of an earlier American captain, Samuel Hall, who held American letters of marque back in the eighteenth century and specialized in raiding the Nova Scotia settlements during the American War of Independence. Hall's Harbour, named for this privateer, is a small cove near Haut Isle where Hall moored his armed sloop during his final raid on the Cornwallis Valley in 1778. When Hall's sloop, the *Mary Jane*, was captured by the British, the captain's strongbox was missing. There can be no doubt that Hall had treasure of a sort, valuables collected during his raids on the colony. It was widely assumed that he had concealed his strongbox ashore in the vicinity of Hall's Harbour, with a cache of such things as money and silverplate, and perhaps some rings and other jewellery.

Just after the Second World War some old documents relating to Hall's life were discovered in the United States, and a party of American treasure hunters believed they had reason to hope his treasure might be found on Haut Isle. They fitted out a small expedition and visited the difficult little island in the early 1950s. They reported later in the American press that they had found very little for their trouble — no treasure, but part of a human skeleton and one ancient coin which (they reported) was clutched in the skeleton's fingers. They sold their story and pictures of their find to *Life* magazine.

There was nothing whatever to connect this "headless skeleton" with Samuel Hall or his supposed treasure or, for that matter, with Mogul Mackenzie and the loss of his pirate vessel some seventy-seven years later. From that wreck or from another wreck at some other time, a single sailor had been washed into the cleft of the cliffs or had managed to clamber up the rocks, only to die there, and had left his bones to bleach in sun and rain, the single coin that he carried in his pocket remaining with his skeleton, while his clothing, along with his flesh and his skull, disappeared into the sea.

AFTERWORD

I T IS WITH SOME RELIEF that it is time to "lay down
the pen," having completed a survey of piracy and privateering in Canada, an aspect of our history never before
fully explored. These pages have attempted to capture some
of the colour, excitement, and pathos so often edited out of
the three and a half centuries of Canadian history preced-
ing World War II. It is with hope that this book has struck
a blow at the myth of Canada's dull past: Canadian history
is vibrant, exciting, and sometimes bloodstained. That
Canadians do not exalt the bloodletting may well be a point
in our favour. Pirates and privateers were common enough
in our past, but Canadians have resisted the temptation to
make heroes of them. We tend to romanticize such idealists

— once they are safely out of the way.

If there is anything to be learned from the lives of the pirates, it is that crime often pays handsomely — not for everyone, of course, only for those who can perform on a grand scale. We have seen pirates who became noblemen and admirals, and one who not only founded a landed family but also became a judge.

Pirates often ended their lives on the gallows. We have seen one die in battle on the deck of his ship and another with an axe buried in his skull. But the danger of such mishaps was no greater than the risks run by any soldier of fortune. The prospect of possible but unlikely retribution deterred none but the timid.

By the middle of the nineteenth century privateering was a thing of the past, and by the end of that century piracy was almost a thing of the past, confined to the Red Sea and the Gulf of Siam. And then, as western civilization began to break down, the well-policed world ceased to have such a comfortable appearance. By the late twentieth century, with the resurgence of the drug trade, piracy was common once more, not only in distant and perilous seas, but right on the doorsteps of North America in the shipping lanes of the Pacific and the Atlantic.

The kind of piracy practised by drug smugglers is quite different from that practised by Easton or Roberts. It usually involves a sneak attack on a private yacht, which is then converted to a drug runner. Wholesale murder is not always necessary in piracy of this sort. Sometimes a pirate may have to dispose of some unlucky yachtsmen by dumping their bodies at sea. Usually the ship is simply stolen without violence from some anchorage among the tropical islands. Hijacking of drug cargoes is another form of modern-day piracy. Rivalries involving smugglers at sea have resulted in sporadic underworld warfare, but violence has not reached the levels that enlivened the liquor trade in the days of Prohibition.

Perhaps the whitewash of Canadian history has reversed the social process that in other countries turned pirates into national celebrities. For nearly 350 years the regions of North America that now make up Canada bred or played host to a succession of sea dogs. An occasional monument recalls their exploits. A few novelists, playwrights, and film-makers have dramatized versions of their stories, and in certain areas where the oral tradition has not totally died away, brave and evil men live on in local yarns and legends. Their names, unlike those of English and American desper-adoes, have not become so familiar to the public that they are used as gimmicks in advertising campaigns. The pirates of Canada remain, as no doubt they should, haunting shad-ows in our nation's past.

BIBLIOGRAPHY

Beirne, Francis E. *The War of 1812*. New York: E.P Dutton, 1949.

Boatner, Mark, ed. *Encyclopedia of the American Revolution*. New York: McKay, 1966.

Bradlee, Francis B. C. *Piracy in the West Indies and its Suppression*. Salem, Mass.: The Essex Institute, 1923.

Calnek, W. A. *The History of the County of Annapolis*. Halifax: Mika Publishing Company, 1897, (reprint) 1980.

Chapelle, Howard I. *The History of the American Sailing Navy: The Ships and their Development*. New York: Bonanza Books, 1949.

Clark, William B. *George Washington's Navy*. New Orleans: Louisiana University Press, 1960.

Champlain Society. *Works of Samuel de Champlain*. Toronto: Champlain Society, 1936.

Defoe, Daniel (Captain Charles Johnson). *A General History of the Pirates*. Edited by Phillip Gosse. London: Printed by P. Sainsbury at the Cayne Press, 1724.

Dupuy, Trevor, and Hammerman, Gay, eds. *People and Events of the American Revolution*. New York: R.R. Bowker, 1974.

Gosse, Phillip. *The History of Piracy*. New York: Longmans, Green and Co., 1932.

Hakluyt, Richard. *The Principall navigations, voiages and discoveries of the English nation, made by sea or overland...* London: Imprinted by George Bishop, Ralph Newberie, and Christopher Barker, 1598–1600.

Horwood, Harold. *Pirates in Newfoundland in the 17th, 18th, and 19th Centuries*. St. John's: Newfoundland Historical Society, 1967.

Horwood, Harold & Butts, Ed. *Pirates and Outlaws of Canada 1610–1932*. Toronto: Doubleday Canada, 1984.

Kirke, Henry. *The first English conquest of Canada, with some account of the earliest settlements in Nova Scotia and Newfoundland*. London: S. Low, Marston and Co., 1908.

Leef, John. *The Atlantic Privateers*. Halifax: Petheric Press, 1978.

———. *A Bluenose Privateer of 1812*. Nova Scotia Historical Quarterly, Vol. III, No. 1.

Legget, Robert. *Ottawa Waterway, Gateway to a Continent*. Toronto: University of Toronto Press, 1975.

Macdonald, Helen G. *Canadian Public Opinion on the American Civil War*. New York: Columbia University Press, 1926.

MacMechan, Archibald. *Sagas of the Sea*. London: J.M. Dent & Sons, 1923.

———. *The Nova Scotia Privateers*. Toronto: Ryerson, 1930.

Mainwaring, Sir Henry. "Of the Beginnings, Practices, and Suppression of Pirates." Unpublished Ms. British Museum, London (c. 1620).

McLennan, J. S. *Louisbourg from its Foundation to its Fall*. London: Macmillan, 1918.

———. *The Life and Works of Sir Henry Mainwaring*. Edited by G. E. Mainwaring. London: Navy Records Society, 1920–1922.

Mason, John. *A brief discourse of Newfoundland*. Edinburgh: Andro Hart, 1620.

Ormsby, W., ed. *The Grey Journals and Letters: Crisis in the Canadas 1838–1839*. London: Macmillan U.K., 1965.

Prowse, D. W. *A History of Newfoundland*. London: Macmillan U.K., 1895.

Radisson, Pierre Esprit. *Voyages of Pierre Esprit Radisson*. Edited by Gideon D. Scull. Boston: Print Society of Boston, 1885.

Shortis, H. T. "Historical Sketches: Harbour Grace." Unpublished Ms. Gosling Memorial Library, St. John's, Nfld. (c.1910).

Smallwood, Joseph R., ed. *The Book of Newfoundland, Vol. 2*. St. John's: Newfoundland Book Publishers, 1937.

——. *The Encyclopedia of Newfoundland and Labrador, Vols. 1–5*. St. John's: Newfoundland Book Publishers (1967) Ltd., 1981–1994.

Snider, Charles Henry. *Under the Red Jack: Privateers of the Maritime Provinces of Canada in the War of 1812*. London: Hopkinson, 1928.

Vaughn, Sir William (*Orpheus* junior). *The golden fleece divided into three parts, under which are discovered the errours of religion, the vices and decayes of the kingdome, and lastly the wayes to get wealth, and to restore trading so much complyned of...* London: Printed for Francis Williams, 1626.

Whitbourne, Richard. *Discourse and Discovery of the New-Found-Land*. London: F. Kyngston for W. Barret, 1620.

Winks, Robin W. *Canada and the United States: The Civil War Years*. Montreal: Harvest House, 1971.

INDEX